Table of Contents

Lesson 1   Finding Main Idea 4

Lesson 2   Recalling Facts and Details 14

Lesson 3   Understanding Sequence 24

Lesson 4   Recognizing Cause and Effect 34

Lesson 5   Comparing and Contrasting .44

Lesson 6   Making Predictions 54

Lesson 7   Finding Word Meaning in Context 64

Lesson 8   Drawing Conclusions and Making Inferences 74

Lesson 9   Distinguishing Between Fact and Opinion 84

Lesson 10   Identifying Author's Purpose 94

Lesson 11   Interpreting Figurative Language 104

Lesson 12   Summarizing 114

Review 1–12 124

Finding Main Idea

Learn About Finding Main Idea

Thinking about the strategy

Authors usually want you to understand one **main idea** about a topic. The main idea is the most important point of a paragraph or of a longer selection. The topic is what the paragraph or selection is all about.

The author may state the main idea in a main idea sentence. When the main idea is stated in a main idea sentence, all the other sentences in the paragraph or selection support or relate to the main idea sentence.

Sometimes, the main idea is not stated. Then you have to figure out the one important point that all the details together make about the topic.

To find the main idea of a paragraph
- Look for a main idea sentence. It is often the first or last sentence of the paragraph.
- Figure out the one main point that all the sentences together make about the topic.

To find the main idea of a selection
- Look at the title and any other headers.
- Look at the first or last paragraph. It often tells the main idea.
- Think about the main ideas of all the paragraphs.

Studying a model

Read the paragraph and the notes beside it.

The topic is weather in New England.

The first sentence states the main idea: the weather in New England changes often and fast in the spring.

All the other sentences give details that show how often and how fast the weather can change.

The weather in New England changes often and fast in the spring. One moment, rain is pouring down. Then before you can find your umbrella, the sun is shining. Ten minutes later, clouds thicken. The sky turns gray. The temperature drops, and soon snowflakes fall. While you're digging your boots out of the closet and looking for the shovel, the temperature rises. The snow melts. The clouds disappear, and the sun reappears. Don't put the boots or umbrella away yet. Remember, this is spring in New England. Who knows what might happen next!

Learn About a Graphic Organizer

Understanding a main idea chart

A **main idea chart** will help you identify the main idea of a paragraph or of an entire selection. You can use a main idea chart when reading news and magazine articles, essays, and other nonfiction and fiction selections.

Here is a main idea chart for the paragraph on page 4. The chart shows the topic, the main idea, and the details that help explain the main idea.

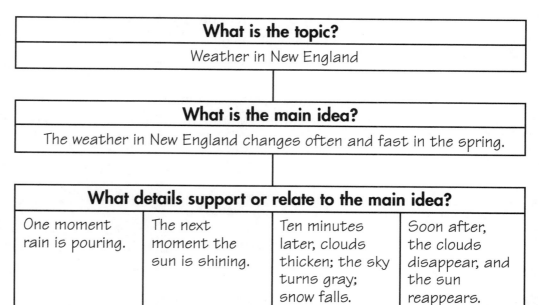

What is the topic?			
Weather in New England			

What is the main idea?			
The weather in New England changes often and fast in the spring.			

What details support or relate to the main idea?			
One moment rain is pouring.	The next moment the sun is shining.	Ten minutes later, clouds thicken; the sky turns gray; snow falls.	Soon after, the clouds disappear, and the sun reappears.

When you complete a main idea chart, you recognize how an author organizes ideas in a paragraph or in an entire selection to make a point.

What is the one point the author wants to make about weather in New England? How does the author communicate this point?
The first sentence of the paragraph clearly states that the weather in New England changes often and fast in the spring. The author then describes in a humorous way how many different kinds of weather you might experience in a short time.

As you read, ask yourself

- What is the main idea of the paragraph or entire selection?
- Is the main idea stated in a main idea sentence?
- What one main point do all the sentences or paragraphs make?

Learn About a Form of Writing

A **feature story** is a news article that focuses on a person or other topic of interest to many readers. Unlike a news story, a feature story examines a topic from a variety of viewpoints.

A feature story often has these elements.

- The headline grabs the readers' attention.
- It may be divided into parts. Each part has its own focus, or main idea, with its own catchy headline.
- It may be presented in a series, over a period of days or weeks.

Here is the opening paragraph of a feature story. As you read, notice how the author uses the headline to draw readers to the story.

> ## Watch Out World! Here Comes Mikey!
>
> Like most fourth graders at Emory Elementary School, Mikey Solo leaves home each weekday morning carrying a backpack filled with books, homework papers, and his lunch. Like the other children, Mikey plays catch or tag while waiting for the school bus. In his jeans, T-shirt, and fleece vest, Mikey does not stand out. But make no mistake: Mikey is not your ordinary fourth grader.

You can use a main idea chart to find the main idea of a part of a feature story or of the entire feature story. Here is a filled-in main idea chart for the opening paragraph above.

What is the topic?			
Mikey Solo			

What is the main idea?			
Mikey appears to be an ordinary fourth grader.			

What details support or relate to the main idea?			
He goes to school each weekday.	He carries books, homework, and lunch in his backpack.	He plays catch or tag while waiting for the bus.	He wears regular clothes: jeans, T-shirt, and fleece vest.

Prepare for the Reading Selection

Gaining knowledge The English language borrows many of its words from other languages. These words have become so common that you may not realize that they came from other cultures. Examples include such words as *squash* (Native American), *courage* (French), *volcano* (Italian), *canary* (African), *kayak* (Eskimo), and *canyon* (Spanish). Many other English words come directly from the ancient languages of Greece and Rome. An example is the English word *phobia*, meaning "an unexplainable fear." The word *phobia* and the word part *–phobia* come from the Greek language. In Greek, the word *phobos* means "fearing." The selection you will read on the following pages is all about fears, which scientists and researchers often refer to as phobias.

Learn Vocabulary

Understanding vocabulary The boxed words below are **boldfaced** in the selection. Learn the meaning of each word. Then write the word that could replace the underlined word or words in the sentence.

overcome	1. That pesky mosquito is <u>bothering</u> me. _____
annoying	2. You can use two <u>ways</u> to find the answer. _____
sensible	3. Please do not <u>get in the way</u>. _____
exposed	4. She tried hard to <u>conquer</u> her shyness. _____
source	5. The plumber found the <u>cause</u> of the leak in a pipe under the sink. _____
interfere	6. Three children in the class have chicken pox, and several more were accidentally <u>unprotected from its effects</u>. _____
methods	7. Cal's good <u>outlook</u> about sports has rubbed off on his teammates. _____
attitude	8. We knew Paula's idea would work because it was so <u>reasonable</u>. _____

Read the first part of the feature story "Fear and Superman."

Fear and Superman

Knowing Fear

"I'm not afraid of anything!"

You've probably heard someone make this boast. Perhaps you have been bold enough to make such a statement yourself. Yet even the comic strip superhero Superman was afraid of kryptonite, that glowing green matter from the exploded planet Krypton. Kryptonite weakened Superman's superpowers and threatened his life.

Some people believe that everyone is afraid of something. According to the list of fears, or phobias, that appeared in a national magazine recently, there do seem to be enough fears to go around. Ranging from A to Z, the list is so long you might develop a fear of finding out you have a fear just by looking at the list.

Fears, however, are not funny, especially to the people who have them. Fears keep people up at night. Fears stop people from going places. Fears cause people embarrassment and worry. Some people spend so much time being afraid that they can't do anything else. When fears get this bad, people usually have to see a doctor who can help them **overcome** their fears.

If you suffer from a fear that stops you from living a healthy, happy life, tell your parents, teacher, or another caring adult.

However, if like millions of other people, you have a fear that is more **annoying** than life-stopping, you have two choices. You can learn to live with your fear. Or, you can try to get over your fear.

Healthy Fear

Is having fear ever **sensible**? Is it silly to have fears? Was Superman silly to fear kryptonite?

Superman knew that kryptonite could destroy him. He did his best to avoid being **exposed** to kryptonite. You might call Superman's fear of kryptonite a healthy fear. By avoiding kryptonite, Superman stayed healthy.

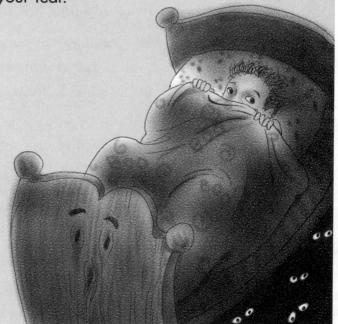

People have healthy fears, too. These fears keep people from doing things that could threaten their lives. Lightning is a powerful, natural force that can injure and even kill. The best way to avoid being hurt by lightning is to avoid being exposed to lightning. Is it silly to be afraid of lightning? If your fear of lightning makes you shake and sweat at the first sign of a cloud in the sky, you probably need help dealing with this fear. If, however, your fear of lightning simply keeps you inside during a lightning storm, then your fear is actually helping to keep you safe. You have a healthy fear of lightning.

Completing a main idea chart

Some of the main idea chart has been filled in. Finish filling in the chart with details from the section "Knowing Fear." Use another piece of paper to create a main idea chart for the section "Healthy Fear."

What is the topic?
Knowing Fear

What is the main idea?
All people have fears that they deal with in different ways.

What details support or relate to the main idea?			
Even the comic strip superhero Superman is afraid of kryptonite.	A recent magazine article had a long list of fears that ranged from A to Z.		

Reading Selection—Part Two

Reading Selection—Part Two

Read the second part of the feature story "Fear and Superman."

Dealing With Fear

People suffer from many different fears and with different degrees of seriousness. How you deal with your fears often depends on the kind of fear you have and how seriously it affects your life.

Learning to live with fear may be easy if you suffer from something like *lutraphobia* (a fear of otters) or *zemmiphobia* (a fear of the great mole rat). Just stay away from otters and great mole rats.

Learning to live with your fear becomes difficult if the **source** of your fear is more common, such as insects (*entomophobia*) or high places (*acrophobia*). In cases like these, decide how serious your fear is. If the sight of an ant or of a tall building makes you shiver but nothing else, then you probably can manage this fear on your own. If, however, you break out in a sweat, shake uncontrollably, scream, or faint just from looking at a picture of a grasshopper or being near a staircase, then your fear is serious. You need to ask for help. Otherwise, you should probably avoid damp dark places where insects breed and, of course, stay off rollercoasters.

You can also try to get over your fear. Remember, we are talking about annoying fears that can **interfere** with the enjoyment of life; we are not talking about paralyzing, life-stopping fears.

People are often afraid of what they don't know. One way to overcome a fear is to learn more about the source of the fear. What if you have a fear of spiders (*arachnophobia*)? Reading about spiders and understanding the part they play in nature might help erase some of your fear. Examining a spider's web might help you appreciate spiders. You probably won't run out and get a pet tarantula, but you may not run and hide the next time a spider crawls up the wall.

Sharing your fears with others can also help. Finding out that someone else has the same fear often makes it easier to deal with fear. You may also learn how other people have gotten over their fears. These **methods** might help you get over your fears or face them with a new **attitude**.

Name That Fear

Some fears and their names are familiar to many people, such as *claustrophobia* (a fear of close spaces) and *acrophobia* (a fear of heights). Other names are less well known, but the fears are common, such as *achluophobia* (a fear of darkness) and *pteromerhanophobia* (a fear of flying). Some names, on the other hand, are rarely used and sound quite strange, although supposedly the fears are real. Here are some of those names:

arachibutyrophobia—a fear of peanut butter sticking to the roof of the mouth

coulrophobia—a fear of clowns

hippopotomonstrosesquippedaliophobia—a fear of long words

genuphobia—a fear of knees

papyrophobia—a fear of paper

telephonophobia—a fear of telephones

xanthophobia—a fear of the color yellow or the word *yellow*

Using a main idea chart

Use details from the section "Dealing With Fear" to fill in the main idea chart. Use another piece of paper to create a main idea chart for the section "Name That Fear."

What is the topic?

What is the main idea?

What details support or relate to the main idea?			

Check Your Understanding

Think about what you've read. Then answer these questions.

1. From the information in the feature story, you could predict that if Superman was near kryptonite,
   Ⓐ he would lose his power to fly.
   Ⓑ he would start to glow.
   Ⓒ he would explode.
   Ⓓ he would start to laugh.

2. Which of these is not an opinion?
   Ⓐ Some people believe that everyone is afraid of something.
   Ⓑ Fears are not funny.
   Ⓒ You can learn to live with your fear.
   Ⓓ Lightning can injure and even kill.

3. When people overcome their fear, they
   Ⓐ think over their fear.
   Ⓑ get over their fear.
   Ⓒ write about their fear.
   Ⓓ pass out from fear.

4. According to the feature story, which of these is not a result of fear?
   Ⓐ lack of sleep
   Ⓑ worry
   Ⓒ embarrassment
   Ⓓ good sense

5. Which of these best tells the main idea of the section "Healthy Fear"?
   Ⓐ Superman knows how to stay healthy.
   Ⓑ Lightning is dangerous.
   Ⓒ Some fears keep people from doing things that can hurt them.
   Ⓓ It is silly to be afraid of lightning.

6. From the information in the section "Dealing With Fear," you can conclude that
   Ⓐ some fears are more serious than others.
   Ⓑ everyone is afraid of tarantulas.
   Ⓒ rollercoasters are dangerous.
   Ⓓ spiders make good pets.

7. If you understand the source of a fear, you know
   Ⓐ the scientific name of the fear.
   Ⓑ how to get over the fear.
   Ⓒ the cause of the fear.
   Ⓓ how many people suffer from the same fear.

8. Which word in Part Two gives a clue to the meaning of the word *paralyzing*?
   Ⓐ enjoyment
   Ⓑ life-stopping
   Ⓒ avoid
   Ⓓ examining

9. Which of these is not a fear named in the feature story?
   Ⓐ a fear of insects
   Ⓑ a fear of otters
   Ⓒ a fear of doctors
   Ⓓ a fear of heights

10. At the end of the section "Dealing With Fear," the word *methods* means
    Ⓐ "new beginnings."
    Ⓑ "long talks."
    Ⓒ "friends and relatives."
    Ⓓ "ways of doing something."

11. Which sentence best states the main idea of the section "Dealing With Fear"?
   Ⓐ How you deal with fear depends on the kind of fear and how it affects your life.
   Ⓑ Learning to live with fear is impossible for most people.
   Ⓒ People who have fears cannot find enjoyment in life.
   Ⓓ People are afraid of what they don't know.

12. What might you do to overcome a fear of spiders?
   Ⓐ Get a tarantula.
   Ⓑ Hide when you see a spider.
   Ⓒ Learn facts about spiders.
   Ⓓ Avoid places where spiders might be found.

Extend Your Learning

- *Write a Letter*

   Imagine that a friend has written to you about a fear. Write a letter to your friend with advice on how to live with the fear or how to overcome the fear. Use ideas from the feature story and from your own experience. When you write your letter, keep your friend's feelings in mind.

- *Read a Feature Story*

   Use the library's on-line catalog to find a newspaper or magazine feature story on a topic that interests you. As you read the story, jot down notes in a main idea chart. Then use the chart to retell the main points of the story to a partner.

- *Finish a Feature Story*

   Look back at the opening paragraph of the feature story "Watch Out World! Here Comes Mikey!" on page 6. What do you think makes Mikey special? Has he invented something? Did he start his own company? Is he a computer whiz or a musical genius? Use your imagination to come up with ideas about Mikey for the rest of the feature story. In a group, decide how to organize ideas into a two-part feature story. Choose details that will appeal to readers and keep them interested. Create a catchy title for each section. Then write your story and share it with the class.

Recalling Facts and Details

Learn About Recalling Facts and Details

Thinking about the strategy

When you read, look for **facts and details** that provide more information about a topic. Facts and details answer the questions *Who? What? When? Where? Why?* and *How?* Facts and details help you understand the main point an author is trying to make in a paragraph, passage, or selection.

To find facts and details in a paragraph or passage, first identify the main idea. Then look for names, dates, places, and events that help explain the main idea. You will often find such facts and details in dialogue, quotations, examples, lists, and descriptions.

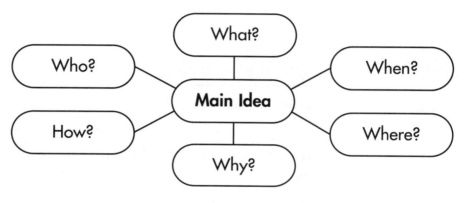

Studying a model

Read the paragraph and the notes beside it.

May 5, 1862, is the day an important battle was fought in Mexico.

Details about Napoleon, General Zaragoza, and their troops give background information.

The main idea of this paragraph is the history of Cinco de Mayo.

In 1862, Emperor Napoleon the Third sent troops to conquer Mexico. On May 5 of that year a small band of Mexican soldiers, led by General Ignacio Zaragoza, defeated the French army in the Battle of Puebla. The Mexican victory was remarkable because the French army was larger and better equipped for battle. France was still able to take control of Mexico, but the battle at Puebla became famous.

Now every year, on May 5, Mexicans and Mexican-Americans in Mexico and the United States gather to celebrate Cinco de Mayo. The words *cinco de mayo* are Spanish for the fifth of May.

Learn About a Graphic Organizer

Understanding a facts and details web

A **facts and details web** will help you organize the facts and details that an author uses to explain a topic so that you can recall these facts and details later. You can use a facts and details web to take notes when you read magazine articles, essays, textbook articles, and other nonfiction and fiction selections.

Here is a facts and details web for the paragraph on page 14. It shows the main idea of the passage and the facts and details that support and explain the main idea.

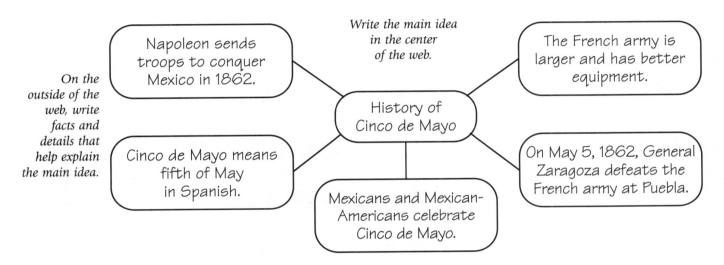

On the outside of the web, write facts and details that help explain the main idea.

Write the main idea in the center of the web.

Napoleon sends troops to conquer Mexico in 1862.

The French army is larger and has better equipment.

History of Cinco de Mayo

Cinco de Mayo means fifth of May in Spanish.

On May 5, 1862, General Zaragoza defeats the French army at Puebla.

Mexicans and Mexican-Americans celebrate Cinco de Mayo.

When you complete a facts and details web, you see how an author has used specific facts and details to explain a main idea. You can then use the completed web to recall facts and details for a test, to write a report, or to retell the main ideas of a selection in your own words.

Why do Mexicans and Mexican-Americans celebrate Cinco de Mayo?
They want to celebrate a famous victory that a small Mexican army had over the French army on May 5, 1862.

As you read, ask yourself

- What is the main idea of the paragraph, passage, or selection?
- What facts and details give more information about the main idea?

Learn About a Form of Writing

Focusing on a magazine article

A **magazine article** presents information about a topic in a lively, interesting way. When choosing topics for a magazine article, authors keep the reading level, interests, and knowledge of their readers in mind. Then they choose examples, quotations, and facts and details that explain the topic in a way that their readers will understand and enjoy.

A magazine article often has these features.

- It contains a variety of facts and details about a topic.
- It has a title that captures the reader's attention.
- It often has subheads that suggest what the following paragraphs are mainly about.
- It may include photographs, maps, diagrams, and other graphic aids.

Here is a paragraph from a magazine article. Notice the catchy title.

Gentle Wooly Creatures

They are gentle and calm and make great pets, especially if you live in the Andes Mountains of Peru, where they have been found for thousands of years. They like to be alone, and they are often shy. If they don't want you around, they might spit to let you know. Their wool is soft and fluffy and is often woven into bright, colorful, warm clothing. What are these gentle wooly creatures? They are llamas, comical-looking members of the camel family.

Organizing ideas in a facts and details web

You can use a facts and details web to organize the facts and details in a magazine article. Here is a facts and details web for the paragraph above.

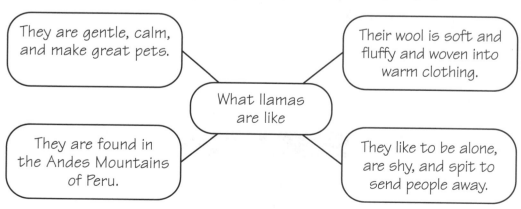

16

Prepare for the Reading Selection

Gaining knowledge
In the magazine article you will read on the pages that follow, you are going to learn about a project that was named for Moses, an important figure in the Bible. According to the bible story, Moses led the Hebrews out of slavery in Egypt to freedom in Canaan, which was later called Palestine. One day, during the long and difficult journey, the Hebrews came to a large body of water. Egyptian soldiers were about to overtake them when God told Moses to lift a rod and spread his arms. When Moses did as God commanded, the waters parted, and Moses and the Hebrews crossed over to the other side. The Egyptian soldiers tried to follow, but as soon as the Hebrews were safe, the waters came together again. The Hebrews were saved from their pursuers.

Learn Vocabulary

Understanding vocabulary

The boxed words below are **boldfaced** in the selection. Learn the meaning of each word. Then write the word that matches the clue.

architecture
industry
disastrous
plagued
devastating
erodes
debris
inflate
complex
stagnant

1. These two adjectives might be used to describe the effects of a terrible storm.

   _____

   _____

2. This word describes something difficult to understand.

   _____

3. This is another word for business. _____

4. This refers to the design of buildings. _____

5. Dirty pond water might be this. _____

6. This means "wears away." _____

7. You do this to a balloon. _____

8. This means "bothered" or "troubled." _____

9. This is trash. _____

Read the first part of the magazine article "Can Venice Be Saved?" by Laura C. Girardi. This article first appeared in *Time for Kids*, April 6, 2001.

Can Venice Be Saved?

Will a high-tech plan keep the ancient city above water?

Gondoliers paddle sleek boats along some 150 narrow canals and under ancient bridges. Singers serenade tourists who stroll along cobblestone streets to admire 15th century **architecture**. Venice, built on 118 islands, is a sparkling gem among Italy's great cities. Its art-filled churches and quaint streets have long made it one of the world's most beloved places. Ten million people visit Venice each year.

People ride gondolas, long narrow boats, through the water-filled streets of Venice. Gondoliers, who use long oars to paddle the boats, often sing as they paddle.

But one of the things that makes Venice so special—its web of waterways—threatens its survival. The water is not just in the lagoon, where it belongs. It's everywhere!

Venice is sinking, and at the same time, the sea around it is rising. In the fifth century, Venetians set the city in the middle of a lagoon to escape enemies. They built it on millions of wooden planks pounded into marshy ground. Since then the buildings have been slowly sinking. The removal of groundwater by local **industry**, a practice that finally stopped in the 1970s, made the city sink even faster. It has dropped more than five inches since 1900.

Meanwhile, global climate changes have raised the world's sea levels by more than four inches this century. For Venice, the combination of sinking ground and rising seas has been **disastrous**.

Water Everywhere

Venice has always been **plagued** by floods. Each year, usually between October and March, strong southeast winds and high tides bring acqua alta (Italian for high water). But as the city sinks and the sea rises, the seasonal floods become worse. The single most **devastating** flood soaked the city on November 4, 1966. Streets and houses were under more than six feet of water! Landmarks and paintings were damaged. Since then, there have been up to 50 floods a year!

Acqua alta **erodes** buildings. The saltwater seeps into bricks and weakens them. Venice's magnificent 900-year-old cathedral, St. Mark's Basilica, now leans slightly to the left because of its unstable foundation.

Experts warn that Venice may sink an additional eight inches in the next 50 years. Already, many citizens are fleeing to dryer spots on Italy's mainland. Many residents have abandoned the first floor of their homes. Few young families with kids remain in Venice.

Maskmaker Lorenzo Pedrocco is staying but says the floodwater is a real pain: "If it gets above a certain level, I have to raise up the refrigerator and furniture so they don't get ruined." Others complain about the smell of the water, which contains waste and lagoon **debris**.

Completing a facts and details web

Some of the facts and details web has been filled in. Add more facts and details that explain and support the main idea in the first part of the magazine article.

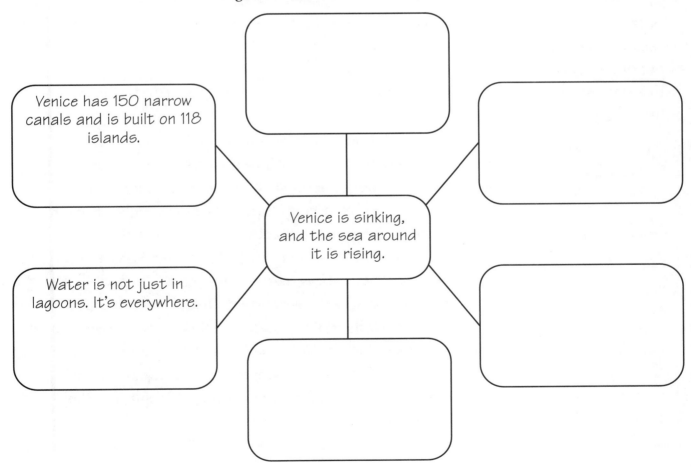

Venice has 150 narrow canals and is built on 118 islands.

Water is not just in lagoons. It's everywhere.

Venice is sinking, and the sea around it is rising.

Read the second part of the magazine article "Can Venice Be Saved?"

Is this a job for Moses?

To save the city, a group called the New Venice Consortium has come up with Project Moses. The $2 billion dam project is named for the biblical figure for whom the Red Sea parted. The plan is to place huge underwater gates at each of the three entrances to the Venice Lagoon. When the water is low, the 79 separate 300-ton flaps would sit on the ocean floor. But when the water rises, the flaps would **inflate** and rise to block Adriatic Sea water.

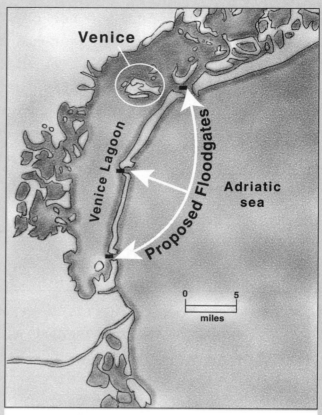

Project Moses: when the Adriatic Sea rises very high, floodgates would inflate and lift up from the ocean floor. They'd keep seawater out of the lagoon and stop flooding in Venice.

The **complex** plan has been in the works for 10 years, but it has yet to win official approval. Environmentalists, in fact, have fought it. They argue that the gates will have to be closed so often that seawater will not be able to move in and out of the lagoon. This will make the lagoon a **stagnant**, dirty pool, harming fish and plants that live there.

Green Parties are political groups that try to protect and improve the environment. Italy's Green Party is among its leading political parties.

Project Moses' fate may be in the hands of Italy's Green Party, an environmentally sensitive political group. Green Party members have suggested other solutions to the high waters. Giorgio Sarto, a Green Party Senator, favors simpler measures, such as continuing to raise streets, restoring eroded parts of the port and cleaning the lagoon. "In order to save Venice, we should first see that the city takes its medicine," he said. "Only as a last resort should it have surgery [like] Project Moses."

Hydraulics is the study of water in motion. Hydraulic engineers study the flow of water. They also design systems that provide flood control.

On March 15 the Italian government decided to continue studying Project Moses. Maria Teresa Brotto, a hydraulic engineer for the New Venice Consortium, is happy. She has argued that smaller steps are not enough: "People want this problem resolved."

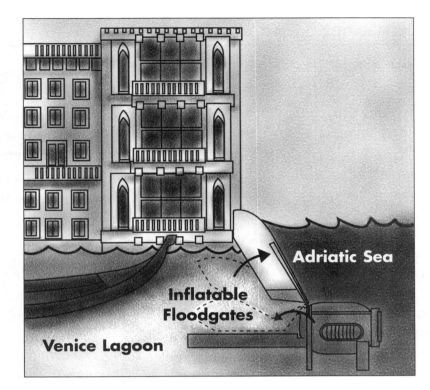

This diagram shows how the flaps of the huge floodgates would inflate and rise to block the water of the Adriatic Sea from entering Venice Lagoon.

Adriatic Sea

Inflatable Floodgates

Venice Lagoon

Using a facts and details web

Fill in the facts and details web for the second part of the magazine article.

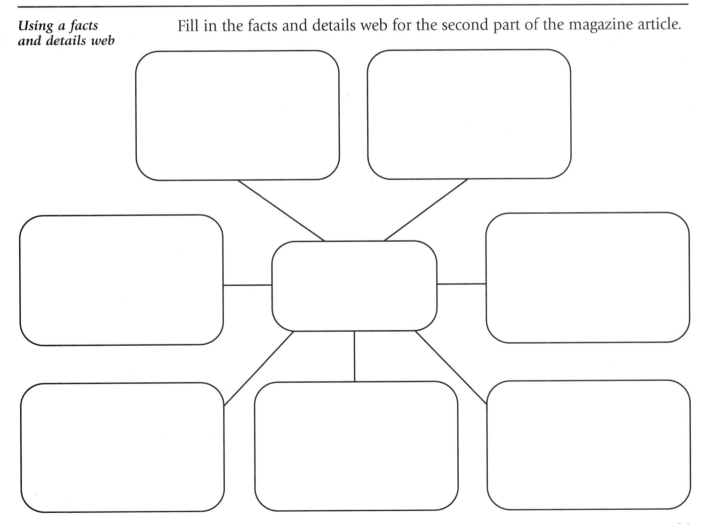

Check Your Understanding

Think about what you've read. Then answer these questions.

1. Which of these is not a detail that the author uses to help you picture the city of Venice?
   - Ⓐ Gondoliers paddle sleek boats along narrow canals.
   - Ⓑ Singers serenade tourists.
   - Ⓒ Tourists stroll cobblestone streets.
   - Ⓓ Global climate changes have raised the world's sea levels.

2. In the magazine article, the author compares Venice to
   - Ⓐ a dirty pool of water.
   - Ⓑ a sparkling gem.
   - Ⓒ a biblical figure named Moses.
   - Ⓓ a cathedral.

3. Venice was built in the middle of a lagoon so that
   - Ⓐ Venetians could escape their enemies.
   - Ⓑ great artists and musicians would live there.
   - Ⓒ Venice would not sink.
   - Ⓓ Venetians could have gondolas.

4. If the removal of groundwater by local businesses had not been stopped in the 1970s, what might have happened to Venice by now?
   - Ⓐ The canals would be dry.
   - Ⓑ Venice would have stopped sinking.
   - Ⓒ Venice might have dropped more than five inches.
   - Ⓓ More tourists would have visited Venice.

5. Because sinking ground and rising seas have been disastrous,
   - Ⓐ Venice has suffered great damage.
   - Ⓑ people enjoy the view.
   - Ⓒ more businesses have come to Venice.
   - Ⓓ there is no groundwater.

6. Since 1966, up to how many floods have there been each year in Venice?
   - Ⓐ 300
   - Ⓒ 118
   - Ⓑ 50
   - Ⓓ 150

7. From the information in the magazine article, you can conclude that
   - Ⓐ Italy's mainland never floods.
   - Ⓑ there are many maskmakers in Venice.
   - Ⓒ there are no children living in Venice.
   - Ⓓ the water in Venice has a bad smell.

8. If the floodgates in the Project Moses plan were to inflate, they would
   - Ⓐ explode into millions of pieces.
   - Ⓑ sink into the sea.
   - Ⓒ fill up with air or gas.
   - Ⓓ lean over.

9. Water that is stagnant
   - Ⓐ is still and often dirty.
   - Ⓑ is healthy for fish and plants.
   - Ⓒ has a fresh, clean smell.
   - Ⓓ rises and falls with the tides.

10. The New Venice Consortium and Italy's Green Party both
    - Ⓐ are in favor of Project Moses.
    - Ⓑ oppose Project Moses.
    - Ⓒ want to save Venice.
    - Ⓓ encourage people to move to the mainland.

11. What is Part Two of the article mainly about?

Ⓐ Italy's Green Party

Ⓑ a biblical figure named Moses

Ⓒ a high-tech plan to stop Venice from sinking

Ⓓ the Venice Lagoon

12. The author wrote this article to

Ⓐ explain why Venice is sinking and the plans to save the city.

Ⓑ describe the art and architecture of Venice.

Ⓒ tell an entertaining story about a city built on a lagoon.

Ⓓ persuade the residents of Venice to move to the mainland.

Extend Your Learning

- *Write a Story About Venice*

  Write a story about living in Venice. With a partner, brainstorm story ideas and the kinds of problems someone your age might have to face living in Venice. Look at the webs you filled in for this lesson. Find facts and details that you can include in your story to make it interesting and realistic. Share your story with the class.

- *Present a Panel Discussion*

  In a group, plan a panel discussion between residents of Venice and city officials of Venice. Use facts and details from the magazine article, and notes from any additional research you do. Write a series of questions and answers that residents and city officials might ask each other in a discussion about how to save Venice. Practice your panel discussion and then present it to the class.

- *Write a Report*

  Use the Internet and other print and on-line resources to learn about another ancient city in Italy, such as Rome or Florence. Jot down facts and details in a web, timeline, or other graphic organizer. Then use your notes to write a report on the city you chose. Include diagrams, charts, maps, and drawings to help make your ideas clear.

LESSON 3 Understanding Sequence

Learn About Understanding Sequence

When you read, you will have an easier time understanding how events are related if you pay attention to when events happen. The order in which events happen is called **sequence**. Authors use sequence to help readers recognize how one event leads to another in a story.

Usually, authors use chronological order, or time order, to present events in a story. Sometimes, however, authors may interrupt a story to tell about an event that happened before the story began. An author might also tell about two events that happen at the same time.

Authors often signal the sequence of events with clue words. Look at the examples in this chart.

WORDS THAT SIGNAL SEQUENCE				
Time Order		**Dates**	**Time of Day**	
first	then	Friday	morning	dawn
second	before	May	afternoon	night
next	after	December 28, 2001	evening	sunset
finally	meanwhile	1492	twilight	dusk

Authors may not use clue words to signal sequence. Then you can determine sequence by asking yourself questions, such as "What happened before or after this event?" or "What happened last?"

Read the beginning of the story and the notes beside it.

The words then *and* after *signal sequence.*

The words two nights ago *signal what happened earlier.*

Lee was almost finished raking the lawn on Saturday morning, and was looking forward to a tall, cool glass of lemonade. Then he spotted something shiny in the grass. He grinned, thinking that it was a quarter or perhaps even a half-dollar. But after he picked up the shiny object, his grin quickly disappeared. Etched on the thin silver disc was the same odd design that he had seen in a dream two nights ago.

Learn About a Graphic Organizer

Understanding a sequence chain

A **sequence chain** will help you keep track of the order in which events occur in a paragraph or in an entire story. You can use a sequence chain to order events in stories, fairy tales, folktales, articles, and essays. You can also use a sequence chain to list the order of steps in a process when reading how-to articles or directions.

Here is a sequence chain for the story beginning on page 24. Notice that the first event in the chain appears last in the paragraph. Since this event happened first in time order, you would list it first in the sequence chain.

List the event that happened first in time.

Tell what happens second, what happens next, and what happens after that.

Tell what happens last in time order.

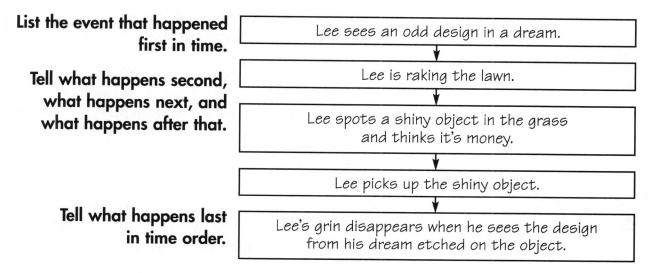

Lee sees an odd design in a dream.

Lee is raking the lawn.

Lee spots a shiny object in the grass and thinks it's money.

Lee picks up the shiny object.

Lee's grin disappears when he sees the design from his dream etched on the object.

When you complete a sequence chain, you understand the order in which events occur in a story. You see clearly how one event leads to another. In this way, a sequence chain helps you understand the relationship of events and ideas in a story.

What happens when Lee picks up the shiny object?
He sees a design on the object. He recalls a dream he had two nights ago. He realizes the design in his dream matches the design on the object.

As you read, ask yourself

- What event happens first in time order? What happens after that?
- What clue words signal the order in which events occur?
- What happens before and after events in a story?
  What events happen at the same time?

Learn About a Form of Writing

Focusing on a fairy tale

One of the most familiar and beloved type of children's story is the **fairy tale**. Who has not heard a version of at least one of the following fairy tales: "Cinderella," "Snow White," and "The Shoemaker and the Elves"?

A fairy tale often combines realistic parts with fantasy, or make-believe, parts. For example, a fairy tale may be set in a realistic place where magical events occur. A fairy tale may have both realistic characters and imaginary characters that do magical things. A story is not a fairy tale if it does not have at least one fantastic or imaginary element.

A fairy tale may also have these special characteristics.

- It often has been retold and passed down over a long period of time.
- It often has a plot in which good characters struggle to overcome evil or mischievous characters.
- The ending often rewards good characters and punishes evil ones.
- Its purpose is to entertain.

Organizing ideas in a sequence chain

As in other stories, the events in a fairy tale are usually presented in chronological order, or time order. You can use a sequence chain to keep track of these events and understand what is happening in the story.

Here is a filled-in sequence chain for events in a familiar version of the fairy tale "Snow White."

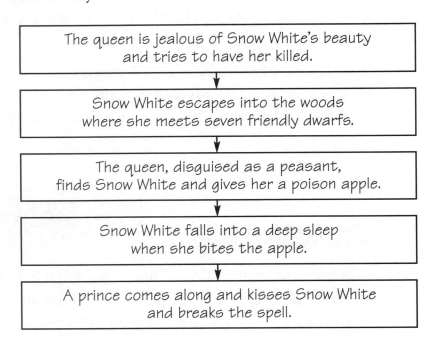

The queen is jealous of Snow White's beauty and tries to have her killed.

↓

Snow White escapes into the woods where she meets seven friendly dwarfs.

↓

The queen, disguised as a peasant, finds Snow White and gives her a poison apple.

↓

Snow White falls into a deep sleep when she bites the apple.

↓

A prince comes along and kisses Snow White and breaks the spell.

Prepare for the Reading Selection

Gaining knowledge

The fairy tale you will read on the following pages is a retelling of a story written in 1844 by the Danish storyteller Hans Christian Andersen. The son of a shoemaker and a washerwoman, Andersen was born in the poor section of Odense, Denmark, in 1805. When he was fourteen years old, Andersen moved by himself to Copenhagen to study the performing arts, but the life of an actor, a singer, and a dancer was not easy. Andersen earned hardly any money and often went hungry. With the help of a friend, Andersen got a scholarship to the Royal Theater so that he could continue his education.

Andersen began his writing career as a playwright and novelist. However, he became famous for his fairy tales. Simple, humorous, and wise, Andersen's fairy tales have delighted both children and adults since they first began to appear in 1835. Among the most famous of his tales are "The Ugly Duckling," "The Emperor's New Clothes," and "The Nightingale."

Learn Vocabulary

Understanding vocabulary

The boxed words below are **boldfaced** in the selection. Learn the meaning of each word. Then write the word whose meaning is similar to the given word.

| exquisite |
| porcelain |
| empire |
| gems |
| mechanical |
| banished |
| hue |
| regain |
| refreshed |
| reveal |

1. jewels _____

2. tell _____

3. recover _____

4. china _____

5. color _____

6. kingdom _____

7. machinelike _____

8. dismissed _____

9. beautiful _____

10. renewed _____

Read the first part of the fairy tale adapted from "The Nightingale" by Hans Christian Andersen.

The Nightingale

The story I will tell you took place very long ago. It is important that you hear this story now before it is forgotten.

The emperor of China was Chinese. The people he ruled were also Chinese. The emperor lived in an **exquisite porcelain** palace. Gardens surrounded the beautiful palace. Beyond the garden walls, there stood a forest. Its tall trees extended all the way to the deep blue waters of the sea. Among the leafy branches of one tree, lived a nightingale. This bird had such a sweet voice that even the busy fishers put down their nets to listen when she sang.

The emperor's city was famous. Travelers from the North, South, East, and West came to admire the beauty of the emperor's palace and gardens. When they heard the nightingale sing, however, they said, "Nothing compares to this!" Back at home, these travelers wrote books, describing the empire. They saved their finest words to tell of the nightingale's song. One of these books found its way to the emperor. He enjoyed reading the glowing descriptions of his **empire**. Yet, when he came to the words, "of all the wonders in the emperor's city, the nightingale is the best," he was puzzled.

"How can this be?" he asked. "I have never heard of such a nightingale!" He called his attendant. "The whole world knows about my nightingale, but I have never heard her sing. Bring me the nightingale," the emperor commanded.

Later that day, the attendant returned empty-handed. "I have looked high and low," the attendant told the emperor. "The story about the nightingale must be false."

"No, no!" the emperor declared. "The great emperor of Japan gave me this book. It contains no falsehoods. Bring me the nightingale tonight!"

The attendant continued his search. This time he found a young kitchen maid who knew the nightingale quite well. The girl led the attendant to the place in the woods where the nightingale lived. When the attendant spotted the little gray bird, he said, "How could such a plain bird cause such a stir?" Then the nightingale began to sing. The attendant was awed by the bird's beautiful voice.

"Dear wonderful nightingale," the attendant said, "please return with me to the palace to honor the emperor with your song."

"The green woods is the best place to hear my song," the nightingale replied. "But I will to come to the palace with you."

The nightingale settled on the perch that had been built for the occasion. Then the emperor gave a sign for the bird to begin singing. The nightingale's song was so sweet that the emperor's eyes brimmed over with tears. Throughout the court, people spoke of the nightingale's song. Some tried to imitate the sound, but of course, none could. The nightingale was so successful, that she was given her own cage at court. She was allowed to fly out twice a day and once a night. For these excursions, twelve servants held twelve silken strings, attached to the nightingale's leg. The nightingale got little joy from these flights.

Completing a sequence chain

Think about what you have read so far. Then fill in this sequence chain for the first part of the fairy tale.

Travelers come to the emperor's city and hear the nightingale.

↓

Travelers return to their homes and write about the nightingale.

↓

The emperor reads about the nightingale in a book and asks that the nightingale be brought to him.

↓

↓

↓

Reading Selection—Part Two

Read the second part of the fairy tale "The Nightingale."

One day, a messenger brought a large package to the emperor. The label said, "The Nightingale." The emperor thought that it was another book written in honor of the nightingale. It was not. It was a wind-up bird from the emperor of Japan. A tag around its neck said, "Japan's nightingale is far better than China's nightingale." The bird was covered with glittering **gems**. When the emperor wound it up, the bird's silver and gold tail moved up and down, and the bird began to sing.

The people of the court were impressed by the **mechanical** bird. They decided to have the real nightingale and the wind-up bird sing together. The two birds did not get along. The real nightingale sang songs of nature. The wind-up bird sang only waltzes. Many people liked the wind-up bird better because of its sparkling beauty. Only later did they notice that the real nightingale had flown back to the green forest.

"Oh, well, what does it matter?" the emperor's attendant said. "We have this beautiful bird who sings just like the real nightingale. One never knew what the real nightingale would sing. With this bird, we know that a waltz is coming."

The emperor allowed his attendant to display the mechanical bird for all the people to hear. Many were dazzled by the bird's outward beauty. Others, like the fishers by the sea, thought its song was not quite right. After the display, the emperor **banished** the real nightingale from the empire. He placed the wind-up bird on silk pillows near his bed. The wind-up bird became number one in the emperor's heart.

Days and months passed. People learned to sing along with the wind-up bird. They knew just when it would click, clack, and whirr. One night, the wind-up bird clicked, clacked, whirred, and popped its springs! Then the music stopped! The doctor put the bird back together, but the bird was worn out and could sing only once a year.

Five years passed, and the emperor became ill. Everyone thought that he would soon die. In his bed, the weakened emperor begged the wind-up bird to sing. But the bird remained silent. Then a sweet song drifted through the open window. The real nightingale had heard of the emperor's illness and had returned.

As the nightingale sang, the emperor's pale color was replaced by a healthy, rosy **hue**. The shadow of death disappeared from the emperor's bedroom. "I banished you from my empire," the emperor said to the nightingale. "Yet you came to help me. How can I repay you?"

"The tears you shed when first you heard me sing are all I ever need," the nightingale said. "Now sleep. **Regain** your strength. I will sing while you sleep."

When the emperor awoke, he felt strong and **refreshed**. "Stay with me," he begged the nightingale. "I will destroy the wind-up bird."

"No," the real nightingale said. "Keep it. I must live in the trees where I can build my nest. If you will let me come when I like, I will come and sing to you of truth, joy, and hope. You must promise me one thing though."

"I promise anything," the emperor said.

"Do not **reveal** to anyone that you have a bird that tells you everything," the bird said. Then the nightingale flew to her home in the woods.

The servants entered the emperor's room, expecting to find him dead. They were startled, therefore, when the emperor sat up and said, "Good morning!"

Using a sequence chain

Use details from the second part of the fairy tale to fill in the sequence chain.

```
┌─────────────────────────────────────────────────────────────┐
│                                                               │
│                                                               │
│                                                               │
└─────────────────────────────────────────────────────────────┘
                              │
                              ▼
┌─────────────────────────────────────────────────────────────┐
│                                                               │
│                                                               │
│                                                               │
└─────────────────────────────────────────────────────────────┘
                              │
                              ▼
┌─────────────────────────────────────────────────────────────┐
│                                                               │
│                                                               │
│                                                               │
└─────────────────────────────────────────────────────────────┘
                              │
                              ▼
┌─────────────────────────────────────────────────────────────┐
│                                                               │
│                                                               │
│                                                               │
└─────────────────────────────────────────────────────────────┘
                              │
                              ▼
┌─────────────────────────────────────────────────────────────┐
│                                                               │
│                                                               │
└─────────────────────────────────────────────────────────────┘
                              │
                              ▼
┌─────────────────────────────────────────────────────────────┐
│                                                               │
│                                                               │
│                                                               │
└─────────────────────────────────────────────────────────────┘
```

Check Your Understanding

Think about what you've read. Then answer these questions.

1. Where does the fairy tale take place?
   Ⓐ at an emperor's palace in China
   Ⓑ at an emperor's palace in Japan
   Ⓒ by the sea at the edge of a forest
   Ⓓ all around the world

2. The emperor's palace was exquisite. It was
   Ⓐ extremely large.
   Ⓑ quite old.
   Ⓒ very beautiful.
   Ⓓ far away.

3. Visitors to the empire had heard the nightingale sing, but the emperor had not. From this, you can draw the conclusion that
   Ⓐ the emperor does not have good hearing.
   Ⓑ the emperor never went into the forest.
   Ⓒ emperors cannot hear the songs of nightingales.
   Ⓓ nightingales sing too softly.

4. What happens after the kitchen maid shows the attendant where the nightingale lives?
   Ⓐ The attendant returns to the emperor empty-handed.
   Ⓑ The emperor commands the attendant to bring him the bird.
   Ⓒ The attendant thinks the stories of the nightingale are false.
   Ⓓ The attendant asks the nightingale to come with him.

5. Which of these does not happen because the nightingale sings so beautifully for the emperor?
   Ⓐ The emperor starts to cry.
   Ⓑ The emperor gets a wind-up bird.
   Ⓒ People try to sing like the nightingale.
   Ⓓ The nightingale is kept in a cage.

6. At the end of Part One, you can tell that the word *excursions* means
   Ⓐ "strings."
   Ⓑ "servants."
   Ⓒ "outings."
   Ⓓ "sounds."

7. The wind-up bird was covered with gems. Which of these are gems?
   Ⓐ feathers
   Ⓑ diamonds
   Ⓒ pebbles
   Ⓓ gold coins

8. A mechanical bird
   Ⓐ has parts that move.
   Ⓑ hatches from an egg.
   Ⓒ builds a nest.
   Ⓓ has soft feathers.

9. Which of these tells one way that the nightingale and the wind-up bird are different?
   Ⓐ Only the nightingale can sing.
   Ⓑ Only the wind-up bird can sing.
   Ⓒ The wind-up bird sings only waltzes.
   Ⓓ The nightingale sings only for the emperor.

10. What happens right after the attendant displays the wind-up bird for all to hear?
    Ⓐ The nightingale and the wind-up bird sing together.
    Ⓑ Everyone notices that the nightingale has flown away.
    Ⓒ The music stops.
    Ⓓ The emperor banishes the nightingale from the empire.

11. Which of these is an important detail that belongs in a summary of the fairy tale?

Ⓐ Gardens surrounded the beautiful palace.

Ⓑ People tried to imitate the nightingale's song, but none could.

Ⓒ The emperor of Japan sent the Chinese emperor a wind-up bird that could sing.

Ⓓ The bird's silver and gold tail moved up and down.

12. What will probably happen after the fairy tale ends?

Ⓐ The nightingale will never sing again.

Ⓑ The emperor will destroy the wind-up bird.

Ⓒ The emperor will reveal that the nightingale tells him everything.

Ⓓ The nightingale will return to the palace to sing for the emperor.

Extend Your Learning

- *Read Another Fairy Tale*

  Choose another Hans Christian Andersen fairy tale. As you read, use a sequence chain to keep track of the order in which events happen in the fairy tale. Then use the sequence chain to retell the fairy tale in your own words to a partner. Discuss how the story might have been different if the events happened in a different order.

- *Make Puppets for "The Nightingale"*

  Use the Internet and other library resources to find directions for making simple puppets. For example, you might choose to make paper-bag puppets. With your group, make puppets for the main characters in "The Nightingale," including the emperor, the attendant, the kitchen maid, the nightingale, and the wind-up bird. Use the sequence chains you filled in while reading the fairy tale to write and present a puppet play of "The Nightingale" for younger classes.

- *Make a Songbird Poster*

  Do research to learn more about nightingales and other songbirds. Use a graphic organizer, such as a main idea chart or a facts and details web to organize information about different kinds of songbirds. Then use your notes to make a poster about songbirds. Illustrate your poster with pictures of songbirds that you draw, cutout, or download from an on-line resource.

LESSON 4
Recognizing Cause and Effect

Learn About Recognizing Cause and Effect

Thinking about the strategy

When you read, you can look for causes and effects to understand why the events in a story happen the way they do. A **cause** is the reason something happens. An **effect** is what happens as a result of a cause.

The plot of a story often consists of a series of causes and effects. One thing happens (the cause) which results in another thing happening (the effect). That effect then becomes the cause of something else happening. Then that effect causes something else to happen. In this way, causes and effects link together and lead to the final outcome of a story.

One way to recognize causes and effects is to look for clue words such as *so, so that, since, because, if, reason,* and *as a result*. However, authors may not use clue words to signal causes and effects. Then you have to think about what happens in a story, why or how it happens, and what you already know about why things happen in real-life situations.

Studying a model

Read the story and the notes beside it.

Jake dropped the open carton of milk is the cause.

You can figure out that the milk spilled from the open carton.

The clue word because signals a cause.

The clue words as a result signal an effect.

It all started when Jake dropped the open carton of milk. He quickly ran to the counter to grab the paper towels to wipe up the mess, but because his back was turned, he didn't see his sister Sylvia come rushing into the kitchen. As a result, he didn't have a chance to warn her to be careful.

"Ow!" Sylvia hollered as she bumped, banged, and slid across the wet, slippery floor. Jake turned to see his sister on the floor, rubbing her right elbow. "I'm all right," Sylvia said to Jake, who looked as if he was going to cry. "Besides, you know what Gramma always says, 'No use crying over spilt milk!' "

Learn About a Graphic Organizer

Understanding a cause-and-effect flow chart

A **cause-and-effect flow chart** will help you identify causes and effects so that you can better understand how the events in a story are linked. You can use a cause-and-effect flow chart to understand cause-and-effect relationships in a variety of fiction and nonfiction selections.

Here is a cause-and-effect flow chart for the story on page 34. It shows how causes and effects are linked in the story. Notice how effects become the causes of other effects.

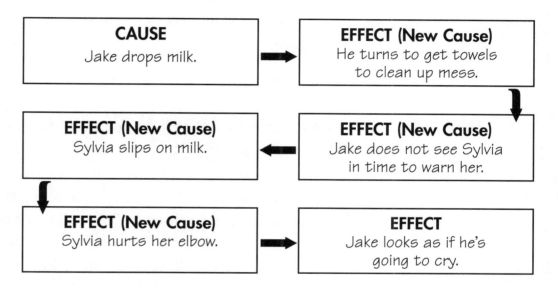

CAUSE
Jake drops milk.

EFFECT (New Cause)
He turns to get towels to clean up mess.

EFFECT (New Cause)
Sylvia slips on milk.

EFFECT (New Cause)
Jake does not see Sylvia in time to warn her.

EFFECT (New Cause)
Sylvia hurts her elbow.

EFFECT
Jake looks as if he's going to cry.

When you complete a cause-and-effect flow chart, you develop a better understanding of how story events are related and how they lead to the final outcome of the story plot.

At the end of the story, why does Sylvia say, "No use crying over spilt milk"? Jake looks as if he's going to cry when Sylvia slips and hurts herself on the wet floor because he's the one who dropped the carton of milk. Sylvia jokes and says, "No use crying over spilt milk" because Jake looks like he's going to cry, and she probably doesn't want him to feel bad.

As you read, ask yourself

- What events cause other things to happen?
- What happens as a result of other events?
- What clue words signal causes and effects?

Learn About a Form of Writing

Focusing on a mystery story

A **mystery story** is a story in which the main characters must use a series of clues to solve a problem. The plot of a good mystery often has twists and turns that add suspense to the plot and that make it more difficult for the main character and the reader to figure out the mystery.

A mystery often has these features.

- It has characters and events that could exist in real life.
- The main character and the reader must identify and use clues within the text to solve the mystery, or problem.
- The problem often focuses on a crime or some other kind of offense.

Here is the opening paragraph from a mystery story.

> Alyssa found the note in her desk at school. It said, "Meet me after school in front of the library. I know about the clock." The note wasn't signed, but the handwriting looked like Tim's. Alyssa didn't know what clock Tim was talking about, but after school she rode her bike to the library. She waited for thirty minutes, then she decided to call Tim from the library's pay phone. All she had was a dollar bill, so she went to the front desk for change. No one was there. No one was anywhere. "It's too quiet in here," Alyssa thought. At the same time she saw the words, "HELP US, PLEASE!" flashing on all the computer monitors.

Organizing ideas in a cause-and-effect flow chart

You can use a chart to identify causes and effects in a mystery. Here is a filled-in cause-and-effect flow chart for the paragraph above.

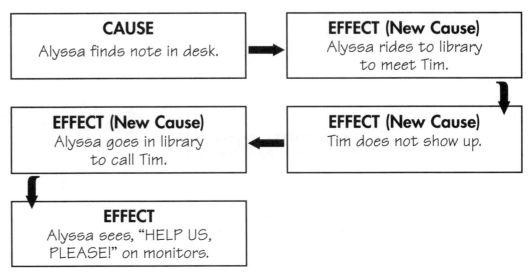

CAUSE
Alyssa finds note in desk.

EFFECT (New Cause)
Alyssa rides to library to meet Tim.

EFFECT (New Cause)
Tim does not show up.

EFFECT (New Cause)
Alyssa goes in library to call Tim.

EFFECT
Alyssa sees, "HELP US, PLEASE!" on monitors.

Prepare for the Reading Selection

Gaining knowledge
In some regions of America, flowering plants grow all year round. In other regions, like the setting of the story you will read on the pages that follow, people wait until late spring to plant most annual flowers. An annual plant lives for a single growing season. Examples of annual flowering plants are geraniums, marigolds, petunias, and pansies. Perennial flowering plants blossom year after year without having to be replanted. Examples of perennials are roses and lily of the valley. Many annuals and some perennials cannot tolerate freezing or near freezing temperatures. Although gardeners are careful to wait until the danger of frost has passed to plant flowering plants, Mother Nature does not always pay attention to the calendar. Occasionally, even in late spring, nighttime temperatures will drop so low that a frost occurs. If plants are not protected from the frost, they can die.

Learn Vocabulary

Understanding vocabulary

The boxed words below are **boldfaced** in the selection. Learn the meaning of each word. Then write the word beside its definition.

| coincidence |
| critters |
| rambling |
| sprucing |
| pun |
| investigate |
| culprit |
| budget |
| flats |

1. someone guilty of a crime or wrongdoing _____

2. another name for animals _____

3. a clever use of words _____

4. making something look neat _____

5. the amount of money someone has to spend

    _____

6. shallow boxes that contain many plants _____

7. look carefully for facts and details _____

8. two similar events happening by chance at the same time

    or in the same place _____

9. wandering from one subject to another when speaking

    _____

Read the first part of the mystery story "The Case of the Missing Flowers."

The Case of the Missing Flowers

Mike and Brittany were in Mike's kitchen when Mike's mom walked in.

"That's odd," Mrs. Moran said to herself, as she rinsed dirt off her hands.

"What's odd, Mom?" Mike asked.

"Well," she said, "I am almost certain that I planted twelve geraniums around the lamppost yesterday, but there are only eleven plants there today."

"That's a **coincidence**," Brittany said. "Yesterday, my mom was all upset because one of her red flowering something-or-others had disappeared."

"Must be some hungry **critters** around here," Mike said.

"I don't know," Mrs. Moran said. "Animals don't usually eat the entire plant . . . Maybe we have a gopher . . . I haven't seen any gopher holes."

"Hey, Mom," Mike said, interrupting his mother's **rambling** thoughts. "We're going to ride our bikes in the circle. I'll be home by dinner."

As Mike and Brittany pedaled down to the circle at the end of his dead-end road, Mike noticed that the neighbors had been busy **sprucing** up their yards.

"Hi, Mr. Ahmad," Mike said, waving to the tall man in front of the white house. Mr. Ahmad was staring at his large flower garden. He was scratching his head and biting his upper lip. Something was puzzling him.

"Is something wrong, Mr. Ahmad?" Mike asked.

"I'm not sure," Mr. Ahmad said. "Well, it's nothing serious anyway. Last week I planted six red petunias and six white petunias. Now there are only five red petunias and five white petunias."

"I feel a mystery blossoming," Mike whispered to Brittany. She groaned at Mike's **pun**, but she agreed that something strange was going on.

"I think this is a case for the Young Crime Solvers," Mike said, as the two friends biked back to his house.

At home, Mike made two phone calls. Within ten minutes, Mike, Brittany, Ben, and Carla were sprawled on the grass in Mike's backyard.

"Here's what we know," Mike said, as he described the details of the Young Crime Solvers' newest case to Ben and Carla.

When Mike was finished, Ben asked, "So, what do we do next?"

"We're going to have to **investigate** to find out who else in the neighborhood has noticed flowers missing."

"Are we sure that the **culprit** isn't an animal?" Carla asked.

"We're not sure of anything right now," Mike said. "Let's split up into pairs. We'll meet tomorrow to compare notes."

For the next hour, Mike and Brittany went door to door asking neighbors about their flowers. They learned that almost every family with a flower garden was missing one or two plants. Mike was careful to write down the name and color of each missing plant in his official Crime Solvers' notebook. He knew that Ben and Carla would do the same.

Completing a cause-and-effect flow chart

Think about what you have read so far. Then fill in this cause-and-effect flow chart for the first part of the mystery story.

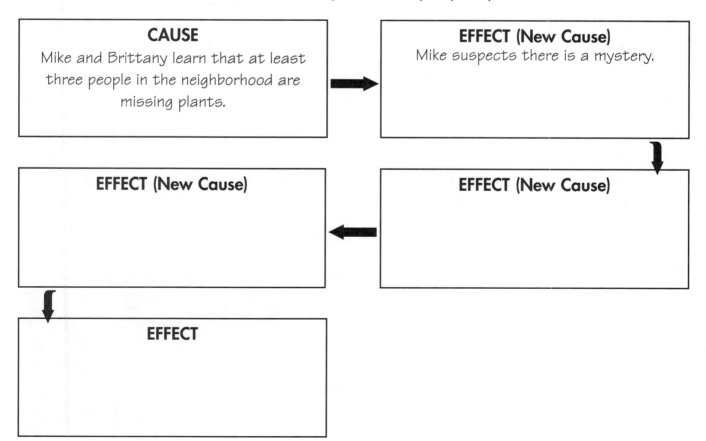

CAUSE
Mike and Brittany learn that at least three people in the neighborhood are missing plants.

→

EFFECT (New Cause)
Mike suspects there is a mystery.

EFFECT (New Cause)

EFFECT (New Cause)

EFFECT

Read the second part of the mystery story "The Case of the Missing Flowers."

The next day, Mike stayed after school to work on his science project. He was going to be late for the Young Crime Solvers' meeting, so he took a shortcut by Mr. and Mrs. D'Elia's yard. He was surprised to see Mrs. D'Elia working in the garden. She hardly left her house anymore, except to see Mr. D'Elia in the hospital.

"Hi, Mrs. D'Elia, how are you?" Mike said. "How is Mr. D'Elia doing?"

"Much better, Michael," she replied. "In fact, he's coming home on Sunday."

"Your garden looks pretty," Mike said, looking at the red and white flowers.

"Well, thank you," Mrs. D'Elia said. "It's small, I know. Flowering plants are much too expensive for my **budget**. I wouldn't have even bothered, but Joseph, I mean Mr. D'Elia, loves having a flower garden."

"Mrs. D'Elia," Mike asked, "do you have all the flowers you planted?"

"No," Mrs. D'Elia said. "I lost two. I should have . . ." A telephone rang inside Mrs. D'Elia's house. "That must be my Joseph," Mrs. D'Elia said, hurrying through the screen door. "He always calls around this time. Good-bye Michael."

Something that Mrs. D'Elia said tugged at Mike's memory. When he got home, his mother was in her garden. "Any more missing flowers, Mom?" he asked.

"No," she said. "But I lost some plants because of last night's unexpected frost."

A light bulb went on in Mike's brain. "That's it!" he shouted.

"You can't be serious!" Brittany said to Mike after she, Ben, and Carla had heard Mike's theory. "You think Mrs. D'Elia stole the flowers! That's nuts!"

"What do all the missing flowers have in common?" Mike asked.

Ben looked at his notes. "They were all either red or white."

"Right!" Mike said. "All the flowers in Mrs. D'Elia's garden are red or white."

"That only proves that she likes red and white flowers," Carla said.

"That's not all," Mike said. "Mrs. D'Elia said she couldn't afford to buy plants."

Brittany said, "Mom said that since Mr. D'Elia got sick, Mrs. D'Elia has been struggling financially."

"Finally," Mike continued, "Mrs. D'Elia said she had 'lost' two plants, not that two plants disappeared. In gardener's language, lost means 'dead, like from frost.'"

"So now what?" Brittany asked. "Are we going over to Mrs. D'Elia's and demand that she return everyone's flowers? She must have really wanted them. She must know that stealing is wrong."

"I have a better idea," Mike said. "Let's talk to my mom."

On Saturday afternoon, Mike rang Mrs. D'Elia's bell.

Mrs. D'Elia was stunned when she opened the door.

"We know how much Mr. D'Elia loves flowers," Mike said. "So we got him a welcome home present."

Tears of joy filled Mrs. D'Elia's eyes as Mike, Brittany, Ben, and Carla carried large **flats** of red and white flowering plants over to her small garden. "I can't accept those," Mrs. D'Elia started to say. "I don't deserve your help. I was wrong to . . ."

"We'll even help you plant them," Mike said.

"Thank you," Mrs. D'Elia said, softly.

"That's okay," Mike said. "What are neighbors for?"

Using a cause-and-effect flow chart

Use details from the second part of the mystery story to fill in the flow chart.

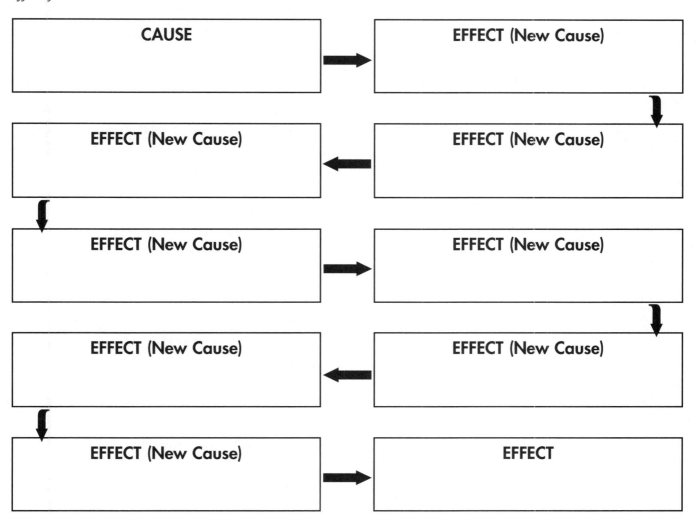

CAUSE		EFFECT (New Cause)

EFFECT (New Cause)		EFFECT (New Cause)

EFFECT (New Cause)		EFFECT (New Cause)

EFFECT (New Cause)		EFFECT (New Cause)

EFFECT (New Cause)		EFFECT

Check Your Understanding

Think about what you've read. Then answer these questions.

1. Which of these appears to be an example of a coincidence?
   - Ⓐ Mike tells his mother that he and Brittany are going to ride their bikes.
   - Ⓑ Mike's mom plants geraniums, and Mr. Ahmad plants petunias.
   - Ⓒ Mike, Brittany, Ben, and Carla live in the same neighborhood.
   - Ⓓ Mike's mom and Brittany's mom are both missing flowers from their garden.

2. From the details in the mystery story, you can draw the conclusion that Mr. Ahmad
   - Ⓐ bites his upper lip when he is puzzled.
   - Ⓑ has petunia plants that have died.
   - Ⓒ has a problem with gophers.
   - Ⓓ wants Mike to help him solve a mystery.

3. Why does Mike make two phone calls after he talks to Mr. Ahmad?
   - Ⓐ He wants to start a crime solving club.
   - Ⓑ He wants to have a meeting of the Young Crime Solvers.
   - Ⓒ He wants to ask Ben and Carla to join the Young Crime Solvers.
   - Ⓓ He wants to play with Ben and Carla.

4. To investigate, Mike will
   - Ⓐ ask questions to get facts.
   - Ⓑ describe a garden.
   - Ⓒ draw pictures of flowers.
   - Ⓓ help his mom.

5. Because Mike stays late after school,
   - Ⓐ his mother becomes worried.
   - Ⓑ he does not meet with his friends.
   - Ⓒ he goes by the D'Elia's yard.
   - Ⓓ he learns that Mr. D'Elia is in the hospital.

6. A budget can help people
   - Ⓐ know what flowers to plant.
   - Ⓑ plan how to spend money.
   - Ⓒ solve a mystery.
   - Ⓓ make friends.

7. What do the words "a light bulb went on in Mike's brain" mean?
   - Ⓐ Mike suddenly understood something.
   - Ⓑ Mike began to think about a problem.
   - Ⓒ Mike turned on a lamp.
   - Ⓓ A part of Mike's brain lit up.

8. In Part Two, you can tell that the word *financially* means
   - Ⓐ "in a difficult way."
   - Ⓑ "having to do with sickness."
   - Ⓒ "having to do with money."
   - Ⓓ "having to do with plants."

9. Which of these is not a clue that Mike uses to solve the mystery?
   - Ⓐ All the flowers in Mrs. D'Elia's garden are red and white.
   - Ⓑ Mrs. D'Elia says that flowering plants are too expensive for her.
   - Ⓒ Mrs. D'Elia says that she "lost" two plants.
   - Ⓓ Mr. D'Elia calls Mrs. D'Elia at the same time every day.

10. What happens the Saturday after the Young Crime Solvers meet for the second time?
   - Ⓐ Mike and his friends take notes about the missing flowers.
   - Ⓑ Mike asks his mother if she is missing any more flowers.
   - Ⓒ Mr. D'Elia comes home from the hospital.
   - Ⓓ Mike and his friends bring Mrs. D'Elia flowers for her garden.

11. What will most likely happen after the mystery story ends?

  Ⓐ Mike and his friends will help Mrs. D'Elia plant flowers.

  Ⓑ Mike's mom will notice flowers missing from her garden.

  Ⓒ Neighbors will call the police about the missing flowers.

  Ⓓ Mrs. D'Elia will buy flowers.

12. The author wrote this mystery story mainly to

  Ⓐ explain how to solve a mystery about flowers.

  Ⓑ describe a pretty flower garden.

  Ⓒ entertain readers with a mystery about missing flowers.

  Ⓓ convince readers that it's difficult to care for a garden.

Extend Your Learning

- *Write a Young Crime Solvers' Mystery*

  With a group, write another story in which Mike and his friends solve a mystery. Read over the features of a mystery story on page 36. Then with your group, brainstorm ideas for the kind of mystery the Young Crime Solvers might solve. You may want to reread "The Case of the Missing Flowers," as well as other mystery stories to get ideas. Use a cause-and-effect flow chart, a story map, or other graphic organizer to plan your story. Then use your filled-in graphic organizer to write your mystery. Share your mystery with the class. Ask classmates to identify the clues that they used to help them solve the mystery.

- *Read a Mystery*

  Read another mystery story of your choice. As you read, use a cause-and-effect flow chart to keep track of story events and clues to the ending. Try to figure out the mystery before the main character in the story does. After you have finished reading, use the filled-in cause-and-effect flow chart to retell the mystery story to a partner. Challenge your partner to figure out the mystery before you get to the end of the story. Be sure to provide all the clues to the mystery in your retelling.

- *Plan a Flower Garden*

  Use the Internet, gardening books, and garden center catalogs to plan a flower garden with six different kinds of flowering plants. You might choose flowers according to their color, size, and how well they grow where you live. When you have decided on what flowers to plant in your garden, draw a picture of it and label the different kinds of flowers. Show the picture to the class and explain why you chose each flower.

Comparing and Contrasting

Learn About Comparing and Contrasting

Thinking about the strategy

Authors often compare and contrast two or more things to help readers understand how people, places, things, or events relate to one another. **Comparing** explains how two or more things are alike. **Contrasting** explains how two or more things are different.

To identify a comparison	• Ask: What things are being compared? How are they alike? • Look for clue words such as *both, same, like, alike,* and *similar*.
To identify a contrast	• Ask: What things are being contrasted? How are they different? • Look for clue words such as *but, unlike, different,* and *however*.

When reading fiction and nonfiction selections, you can look for comparisons and contrasts that the author clearly states. You can also use details in the text to make your own comparisons and contrasts.

To help readers recognize comparisons and contrasts in an informational article, an author may organize details feature by feature. The paragraph below is organized feature by feature. An author may also organize details subject by subject. Then the author writes separate paragraphs that include all the features for each thing being compared.

Studying a model

Read the paragraph and the notes beside it.

Ways sisters are alike: fair skin, green eyes, dark brown hair. Clue words: all, same

Ways sisters are different: height, activities. Clue words: unlike, while

Gina, Lisa, and Maria are sisters. Gina is 11, Lisa is 10, and Maria is 9. All three girls have fair skin and green eyes. Lisa and Maria are average height for their age, unlike Gina, who is tall for her age. While all three girls have the same dark brown hair, Gina and Maria have long, curly hair, while Lisa's hair is short and straight. In their spare time, Gina and Maria enjoy being outdoors, playing sports. Lisa would rather be indoors reading a mystery novel.

Learn About a Graphic Organizer

Understanding a features chart

A **features chart** can help you recognize how two or more things are alike and how they are different. A feature is a special trait. When you fill in a features chart, you identify the features, or traits, of whatever is being compared and contrasted. You can use a features chart to compare and contrast characters, settings, or events in a story, or the characters, settings, or events of several stories. You can also use a features chart to compare and contrast people, animals, places, or events in informational articles, essays, and other nonfiction selections.

To complete some features charts, you make check marks √ or *X*s. For other features charts, like the one below, you jot down notes for each feature. Here is a features chart for the paragraph on page 44.

These heads show who or what is being compared and contrasted.

In this column, list the features that you will compare and contrast.

Feature	Gina	Lisa	Maria
Skin	fair	fair	fair
Eyes	green	green	green
Height	tall	average	average
Hair	dark brown, long, curly	dark brown, short, straight	dark brown, long, curly
Activities	outdoors, playing sports	indoors, reading	outdoors, playing sports

Write details for each feature under each head.

When you complete a features chart, you get a clear picture of how two or more things are alike and how they are different. You understand how the things being compared and contrasted relate to one another.

What features do Gina, Lisa, and Maria share?
They all have fair skin, green eyes, and dark brown hair.

As you read, ask yourself

- What is being compared? What is being contrasted?
- How are these people, places, things, or events alike? How are they different?
- What clue words signal likenesses and differences?

Learn About a Form of Writing

Focusing on an informational article

An **informational article** presents facts, details, and examples that help explain a topic. Although an informational article may be on any topic of interest, many informational articles focus on science and nature.

An informational article often has these features.

- It uses facts, details, and examples to explain a topic.
- It may contain photographs, drawings, charts, or other graphic aids.
- Its main purpose is to give information about a topic.

This passage from an informational article describes members of the dog family. The author has organized details subject by subject.

> Wolves are the size of large dogs. Wolves, however, have wider heads, larger feet, longer legs, and bushier tails. Full-grown male wolves weigh about 97 pounds and are about 6 feet long from their snouts to the tip of their tails. The two kinds of wolves are the gray wolf and the red wolf.
>
> Foxes are the size of small, wiry dogs. Foxes have pointed ears and long snouts, and like wolves, they have bushy tails. Full-grown foxes weigh only about 10 pounds and are just $3\frac{1}{2}$ feet long from snout to tail tip. The three kinds of foxes are the Arctic fox, the gray fox, and the red fox.

Organizing ideas in a features chart

You can use a features chart to note comparisons and contrasts in an informational article. Here is a filled-in features chart for the passage above.

Feature	Wolves	Foxes
Compared to average dog	large	small
Special traits	wide heads, large feet, long legs, bushy tails	pointed ears, long snouts, bushy tails
Average weight and length	97 pounds, 6 feet long	10 pounds, $3\frac{1}{2}$ feet long
Kinds	2—gray wolf, red wolf	3—Arctic fox, gray fox, red fox

Prepare for the Reading Selection

Gaining knowledge
For thousands of years, people have been awed by the grace, beauty, and power of lions, tigers, and other members of the wild cat family. Nature has given big cats powerful bodies, strong jaws, and sharp teeth to help them hunt. Many big cats also have special markings on their fur. These markings make the cat difficult to see when it is stalking its prey. While big cats once roamed the earth in large numbers, today some kinds of big cats have become extinct. Sadly, all of the big cats that you will read about in the article on the pages that follow, are endangered or threatened, mostly as a result of human actions.

Learn Vocabulary

Understanding vocabulary

The boxed words below are **boldfaced** in the selection. Learn the meaning of each word. Then write the word that matches the clue.

resemble
unique
retractable
survive
sprint
camouflage
sociable
solitary
muscular

1. This describes something that can be drawn back in.

   _____

2. This describes someone who enjoys being with other people.

   _____

3. This could describe a weightlifter.

   _____

4. You do this when you look like someone else.

   _____

5. This is a run that is short but quick.

   _____

6. This describes someone who likes to be alone.

   _____

7. This describes something or someone that is like no other.

   _____

8. You do this when you live through hard times.

   _____

9. This helps you to blend into the environment.

   _____

Read the first part of the informational article "Big Cat, Wild Cat."

Big Cat, Wild Cat

Big cats have an extended family that, in many ways, is like your extended family. While all big cats **resemble** each other, none looks exactly like another. And each big cat has traits that make it a **unique** member of the cat family.

Tigers are the biggest of the big cats. An adult male tiger can weigh 420 pounds and be 9 feet long. The female tigress weighs about 100 pounds less and is a foot shorter. The tiger's most striking feature is its black-striped, yellow-orange coat. Just as no two people have the same fingerprints, no two tigers have the same stripe pattern. Tigers also have gold-yellow eyes that allow them to see in the dark. They have **retractable** claws that they can pull back when they walk. And, of course, tigers have a fierce roar that can be heard for miles.

Tigers can live in any climate from the steamy jungles of Asia to the frozen forests of Siberia, Russia. As long as tigers have shade, water, and food, they can **survive**. Unlike almost all other big cats, tigers like water and are great swimmers.

A tiger's diet includes deer, wild antelope, and other large animals. Tigers also eat monkeys, frogs, and other small animals. Tigers hunt alone and at night, aided by their keen senses of sight and hearing. Tigers hide in high grass or behind a tree or rock to stalk their prey. When they get as close as they can, they leap and pounce on their prey. Like other big cats, tigers cannot run for a long time. After a **sprint**, tigers must rest.

A group of tigers is called a *streak*. However, male tigers would rather be alone. A tigress, on the other hand, will stay with her cubs until the cubs are about two. Then, the male cubs will usually wander away. Female cubs often stay within their mother's territory.

Lions are perhaps the most popular of the big cats. Like tigers, lions have strong, powerful bodies. However, lions are smaller. Full-grown male lions usually weigh about 375 pounds and are about 9 feet long. The female lioness weighs about 275 pounds and is about 8 feet long. The fur of a lion's coat is a brownish-yellow. This helps to **camouflage** the lion in the grass. Lions also have golden eyes, claws that retract, and a mighty roar.

By far, the most outstanding feature of the male lion is its mane. No other big cat has this thick hood of hair that extends from the lion's head to its shoulders. Some manes are blond. Others may be brown, black, or a mix of all three colors.

Lions can live in cool or hot climates. They are most at home in the grassy plains of India and Africa. Lions are nocturnal hunters who use their sharp senses to find deer, antelope, and other large animals in the dark. Since the lion's body is not built for speed, a lion must sneak up on its prey. To do this, the lion lowers its body and slowly slinks toward its victim. When it gets within 50 feet, it races forward and grabs its prey.

Lions are the most **sociable** of the big cats. They live in groups called *prides* with as many as 30 or 40 other lions. Lionesses usually stay with the pride. Young male lions are often forced out of the pride. When they are grown, they may fight the males of other prides for control of the pride.

Completing a features chart

Fill in the features chart for the first part of the informational article. Some features have been filled in.

Feature	Tiger	Lion
average size	male: 420 lb, 9 ft long female: 320 lb, 8 ft long	male: 375 lb, 9 ft long female: 275 lb, 8 ft long
female	tigress	lioness
coat	yellow-orange with black stripes	brownish-yellow; male has mane

Read the second part of the informational article "Big Cat, Wild Cat."

Cheetahs are the fastest land animals on earth. Some cheetahs have been known to run faster than 60 miles per hour. Cheetahs are built for speed. Their bodies are slender. Their heads are small. Their legs are long. Their paws are narrow, and their claws do not retract all the way. Cheetahs also have large nostrils. This lets them take in plenty of oxygen when they run. However, cheetahs cannot run far without having to stop to rest.

Adult male cheetahs weigh a little more than 100 pounds and are about $6\frac{1}{2}$ feet long. Female cheetahs are smaller. The cheetah's yellowish-brown coat is marked with black spots. One surprising feature of the cheetah is its voice. Cheetahs do not roar. They purr. Sometimes, they yelp like a dog.

The cheetah's habitat includes the grassy plains of Africa and Asia. Like tigers, cheetahs are **solitary** animals. Some males may live with females in groups. A group of cheetahs is called a *coalition*. A female cheetah will have a litter of three to five cubs. Cubs who are not killed by predators stay with their mother for up to eighteen months. Like other big cats, cheetahs stalk their prey. However, because cheetahs usually hunt during the day, they rely on speed to capture small antelope and other medium-sized mammals.

Leopards are large graceful cats. Adult male leopards weigh between 100 and 160 pounds. They are about 8 feet long. The females are about thirty percent smaller. Most leopards have tan-colored coats with black spots. These spots are called *rosettes*. Leopards can have different shades of fur. The color depends on whether the leopards live in the forests, on the open plains, or in the mountains. Some leopards are born with such dark fur that the rosettes are hard to see. These black leopards are often called black panthers.

Leopards inhabit parts of Africa and Asia. A group of leopards is called a *leap*. Like many other big cats, leopards like to be alone. They roar to avoid other leopards.

Leopards usually hunt at night. Their prey includes gazelles, impalas, and other medium-sized animals. Leopards will also eat hares, reptiles, insects, monkeys, squirrels, and whatever else is available. They are not fussy. Leopards are quite strong and are very good climbers. They often carry their prey high into trees to keep it from other animals.

Jaguars are bigger and stronger than any of the other big cats that live in North and South America. Jaguars weigh between 200 and 250 pounds. They may be 5 to 8½ feet long. Jaguars are often confused with leopards because of their similar coats. Like leopards, jaguars have brownish-yellowish fur with dark rosettes. The jaguar's rosettes, however, have smaller dots inside them. Jaguars also have larger heads than leopards. And they are shorter and more **muscular**. Black jaguars are also sometimes called black panthers.

Jaguars live mostly in forests that are near water. They are not social animals and get together only to mate. Like leopards, jaguars roar to avoid each other.

Jaguars usually hunt at night and will eat whatever they can find. Jaguars hunt deer, cattle, turtles, wild pigs, rodents, and other ground animals. A jaguar may climb a tree to hunt monkeys, but the jaguar is not as good a climber as the leopard. The jaguar, however, is a good swimmer and an expert fisher.

Using a features chart   Use details from the second part of the informational article to fill in the features chart.

Feature			

Check Your Understanding

Think about what you've read. Then answer these questions.

1. From this informational article, what can you conclude about big cats?
   - Ⓐ They are all meat-eaters.
   - Ⓑ They are all good swimmers.
   - Ⓒ They do not have good hearing.
   - Ⓓ They live in trees.

2. When tigers sprint, they
   - Ⓐ splash water.
   - Ⓑ get a new stripe pattern.
   - Ⓒ run a short distance very fast.
   - Ⓓ hide behind a tree or rock.

3. What can you predict a two-year-old male tiger cub will do?
   - Ⓐ grow a mane
   - Ⓑ leave its mother
   - Ⓒ drag its prey up a tree
   - Ⓓ get black spots on its fur

4. Which of these sentences from the informational article is an opinion?
   - Ⓐ An adult male tiger can weigh 420 pounds and be 9 feet long.
   - Ⓑ The fur of a lion's coat is brownish-yellow.
   - Ⓒ By far, the most outstanding feature of the male lion is its mane.
   - Ⓓ A female cheetah will have a litter of three to five cubs.

5. In the section about lions, the meaning of the word *nocturnal* is
   - Ⓐ "in the morning."
   - Ⓑ "during the day."
   - Ⓒ "in the afternoon."
   - Ⓓ "at night."

6. In what way are lions different from most other big cats?
   - Ⓐ Lions cannot pull back their claws.
   - Ⓑ Lions are more sociable.
   - Ⓒ Lions stalk their prey.
   - Ⓓ Lions roar.

7. How are cheetahs like some other big cats?
   - Ⓐ Cheetahs are very slow.
   - Ⓑ Cheetahs cannot run for a long time.
   - Ⓒ Cheetah's have short legs.
   - Ⓓ Cheetahs roar to avoid other cheetahs.

8. Big cats who are solitary
   - Ⓐ like to live and hunt alone.
   - Ⓑ are smaller than other animals.
   - Ⓒ sleep in dens.
   - Ⓓ have dark fur.

9. Why must cheetahs rely on their speed to catch prey?
   - Ⓐ Because all their prey is faster than they are.
   - Ⓑ Because they have weak vision.
   - Ⓒ Because they hunt during the day when they might be seen.
   - Ⓓ Because they are not as strong as other big cats.

10. Jaguars are muscular which means that they
    - Ⓐ have well-developed muscles.
    - Ⓑ have natural musical talent.
    - Ⓒ get along well with other animals.
    - Ⓓ fight fiercely and frequently.

11. Which of these is not a group of big cats?

Ⓐ streak

Ⓑ pride

Ⓒ slink

Ⓓ leap

12. What was the author's main purpose for writing this article?

Ⓐ to convince readers that big cats need to be protected

Ⓑ to help readers learn facts about some big cats

Ⓒ to describe how big cats stalk their prey

Ⓓ to entertain readers with a story about lion cubs

Extend Your Learning

- *Write a Play*

  Work with a group to write a one-act play, based on the information in "Big Cat, Wild Cat." You might write a play in which the different big cats meet each other for the first time at a large family gathering in the jungle. Look over the features charts that you filled in for Part One and Part Two of the reading selection to get ideas for what each of the big cats might say to each other. Rehearse your play and present it to the class.

- *Make a "Big Cat, Wild Cat" Poster*

  With a partner, do research to find facts about one other big cat, such as the cougar, lynx, bobcat, or ocelot. You can look in an encyclopedia or search the Internet for information. Then make a poster that compares and contrasts big cats. Include the big cat you researched and at least two of the big cats you read about in "Big Cat, Wild Cat." Look over your completed features charts from Part One and Part Two of the reading selection to decide what kind of information to include in your poster. Display your poster in the classroom.

- *Read More About an Animal Family*

  Use an encyclopedia or search the Internet to learn more about wolves, foxes, and other members of the dog family, such as coyotes and jackals. Or choose another family of animals to read about, such as bears or birds of prey. As you read, fill in a features chart to help you recognize comparisons and contrasts among the different animals. Then use your features chart to write an informational article about the family of animals you chose.

LESSON 6 Making Predictions

Learn About Making Predictions

Thinking about the strategy

Good readers stay interested and involved in a story by **making predictions** about what will happen next. A prediction is a logical, or sensible, guess, based on what the author reveals to you through story clues and what you know from your own life experiences. Of course, you cannot know for sure what will happen next in the story unless you keep on reading.

Follow these steps to make a prediction.

1. Gather story clues about characters, setting, and events.	2. Think about what you already know about the way people or animals act in real life.	3. Make a logical prediction based on story clues and what you know.

Because a prediction is a guess, you do not need to worry about whether your prediction is right or wrong. As you continue to read, you will gather more information about the characters and events. Then you can revise your prediction, add to your prediction, or make a new prediction.

Studying a model

Read the beginning of the story and the notes beside it.

Link is a mean cat who bullies the other cats. I know that bullies cause trouble.

The narrator says there would be trouble between Chance and Link. I know that when a narrator says something, it often happens.

The best thing that I can say about Link is that he was a curious cat. Other than that, he was cranky, bossy, selfish, and vain. In Link's opinion, no other cat was better looking, smarter, or braver. And since Link was the biggest and meanest cat in the alley, none of us dared stand up to his bullying. Then Chance showed up. Chance was not like the rest of us. The moment that she and Link gazed into each other's eyes, I knew there would be trouble.

54

Learn About a Graphic Organizer

Understanding a prediction map

A **prediction map** will help you keep track of story clues and what you know from your own life experiences so that you can make logical predictions. A prediction map can help you make predictions as you read realistic fiction stories, fantasies, fables, personal narratives, and other kinds of fiction and nonfiction selections.

Here is a prediction map for the story beginning on page 54.

List facts and details from the story.

Story Clues	What I Already Know
Link is a mean bully. None of the other cats stand up to Link. Chance was not like the rest of us. I knew there would be trouble.	Bullies cause problems for others. When a story narrator says something might happen, it often happens.

List what you know from your own experiences.

Make a prediction based on story clues and what you know.

Prediction

Link will try to bully Chance.
Chance will stand up to Link and force him to leave.

When you complete a prediction map, you guess what will happen next in a story. Then you read on to check your prediction and find out what happens. In this way, you stay involved in the story. You also understand how characters and events relate to one another in the story.

How can you find out what happens after Chance and Link meet?
You can read on to check your prediction and perhaps make a new one.

As you read, ask yourself

- What clues has the author provided in the story?
- What do I already know about the way real people and animals might act in a similar situation?
- What do I think will happen next?

Learn About a Form of Writing

Focusing on a realistic fiction story

A **realistic fiction story** is a story that has a setting and characters that could exist in real life. The plot of a realistic fiction story develops around events that could really happen.

A realistic fiction story usually has these features.

- It has characters, a setting, and events that are like people, places, and events in real life.
- The story often takes place in the present or the recent past.
- The characters often struggle with problems that people struggle with in real life.

Here is the beginning of a realistic fiction story. Notice that the setting is a real place and the characters are like people you might know.

> Ten-year-old Trahn stood on the train platform with his mother, waiting for the doors of the train to open. "Don't let go of my hand until we are inside," she said. "We mustn't get separated." Trahn nodded, but when the doors opened, the huge mass of people around them began pushing and shoving. Trahn lost his grip on his mother's hand as he was shoved forward.

Organizing ideas in a prediction map

You can use a prediction map to make predictions when you read a realistic fiction story. Here is a filled-in prediction map for the beginning of the story above.

Story Clues	What I Already Know
Trahn's mother says, "We mustn't get separated."	People sometimes get separated in huge crowds.
Trahn lost his grip on his mother's hand.	Being separated from a parent is scary.

Prediction
Trahn will become separated from his mother.
Trahn will be very scared.

Prepare for the Reading Selection

Gaining knowledge

The boy in the story you are going to read loves pizza. He's not alone. Every year, Americans eat an average of 23 pounds of pizza each! More than 61,000 pizza shops in the United States sell about 3 billion pizzas every year! Pizza first came to the United States from Italy in the late 1800s, and most people think of pizza as an Italian food. However, researchers do not all agree on who invented pizza. Some say that pizza was first made in Naples, Italy. Others think that the Greeks invented pizza when they flattened bread dough into a round shape; topped it with oils, cheese, and herbs; and used the rim of the baked crust as a handle. The Greeks later introduced pizza to southern Italy, where the first Italian pizzeria opened in Naples, in 1830. The people of Naples added tomatoes to the Greek dish, and then cheese to create the pizza we enjoy today.

Learn Vocabulary

Understanding vocabulary

The boxed words below are **boldfaced** in the selection. Learn the meaning of each word. Then write the word that answers the question.

| typical |
| preferred |
| interfere |
| commitment |
| assured |
| intense |
| studio |
| posed |
| headquarters |
| expires |

1. Where might a singer record a song? _____

2. What word is the opposite of *carefree*? _____

3. What word is a synonym for *vowed* and *promised*? _____

4. What word means "a promise to complete a job"? _____

5. What kind of day is it if nothing unusual happens? _____

6. Where might a company president have his or her office? _____

7. What word means "comes to an end"? _____

8. What word means "to come between"? _____

9. What verb belongs with *model, photographer,* and *picture*? _____

10. What word suggests that one thing was chosen over another? _____

Read the first part of the realistic fiction story "The Boy Who Loved Pizza."

The Boy Who Loved Pizza

Six months ago, if you had passed Lamont on the sidewalk, you probably would not have shouted, "Look! It's Lamont Carver!" In fact, you probably wouldn't have noticed him, unless he bumped into you. Like a lot of eleven-year-old boys, Lamont didn't always watch where he was going.

Six months ago, Lamont was an ordinary, happy child. He got along with his parents. He only argued every once in a while with his older sister Flo. He did well in school. He enjoyed riding his bike and playing soccer, baseball, and video games with Sam and Ben, his best friends. All in all, Lamont was pretty **typical**, except maybe for one thing. Lamont loved pizza.

You're probably thinking, "What's the big deal?" A lot of people like pizza. Certainly, most youngsters would choose pizza over Brussels sprouts any day. But, Lamont didn't just choose pizza over Brussels sprouts. Lamont **preferred** pizza over ice cream, cake, cookies, candy, and ANYTHING else. If he could have, he would have eaten pizza for breakfast, lunch, and dinner. Of course, Lamont's parents insisted that he eat a balanced diet that included vegetables, fruit, dairy products, and grains, so Lamont did eat other things. However, when he could, he ate pizza. His favorite was plain pizza, well-done with extra cheese, but he wasn't fussy. He would eat any pizza you put in front of him. Lamont loved pizza.

This is why, when Lamont's sister Flo saw the ad in the local paper, she ran into his room, shouting, "Read this, read this!"

"Okay, okay," Lamont said, as he took the paper and read the ad aloud.

> We are looking for a child between the ages of 10 and 14 to be a spokesperson for a new pizza company. If you like pizza and would like to earn money for college, have your parents contact Ms. Camilla Santoro at 555-1001. The job requires some travel that will not **interfere** with school.

"Do you think Mom and Dad would call?" Lamont asked Flo. Visions of large cheese pizzas, hot and crispy, whirled around in his brain.

"I think the part about earning money for college might help convince them. Besides, it can't hurt to ask," Flo pointed out.

Flo had been right. After discussing the idea, Mr. and Mrs. Carver agreed to call Ms. Santoro for more information.

"I don't know anyone who likes pizza more than my son," Mr. Carver told Ms. Santoro over the phone. "Sure, okay, yes, fine, we'll see you then," Mr. Carver said, jotting details on a piece of paper.

"Here's the deal," Mr. Carver told his wife and children after he hung up. "A new pizza company called Pizza With a Heart is opening pizza shops all over the state. They want one child to star in all their television, radio, newspaper, and magazine ads."

Mrs. Carver frowned, "That sounds like a major **commitment**."

"It does," Mr. Carver said. "But Ms. Santoro **assured** me that until school gets out, all the filming and recording will be done on weekends. The summer schedule will be more **intense** as the company begins opening stores across the state. If the pizza chain is successful, the company will be opening stores in other states. The child who gets this job could be a national star!

"Tryouts are Saturday morning at the State Civic Center," Mr. Carver said, turning to Lamont. "You have an 8:00 A.M. appointment. You're going to have to eat a lot of pizza early in the morning. Are you sure you want to do this?"

"Are you kidding?" Lamont said, with a huge grin on his face.

Completing a prediction map

Finish filling in the prediction map for the first part of the realistic fiction story. Predict what you think will happen next in the story. Then turn the page and read on to check your prediction.

Story Clues	What I Already Know
Lamont is eleven years old. He loves pizza.	

Prediction

On Saturday morning, Lamont looked into a television camera for the first time. He wasn't the least bit nervous as he smiled and said, "Hi, I'm Lamont Carver, and I love pizza." Then he reached into a heart-shaped pizza box, slid out a steaming slice of pizza from a heart-shaped pizza, and took a bite. He smacked his lips, looked back at the camera, and said, "Take it from a boy who loves pizza, Pizza With a Heart is the best pizza in town." Then he took another big bite of pizza.

Ms. Santoro looked at the camera person. "The camera loves him," the camera person told Ms. Santoro. "He's a natural." Dozens of children and pizzas later, Ms. Santoro offered Lamont the job as spokesperson for Pizza With a Heart.

Of course, Lamont accepted. And so, every Saturday and Sunday until school got out, Lamont's father or mother drove him to a downtown **studio** where he filmed television ads, recorded radio ads, or **posed** for newspaper and magazine ads. All day, Lamont had to eat pizza. Lamont could not have been happier.

Soon, everywhere Lamont looked, he saw himself eating pizza. On television, in the city newspaper, in magazines, and even on the sides of city buses, there he was with a piece of pizza in his mouth. Ben and Sam called him "pizza boy." Strangers on the street began stopping him to ask, "Aren't you the boy who loves pizza?"

Then school ended for the year. The Pizza With a Heart company began opening pizza shops in towns and cities all over the state. At each grand opening, Lamont was there to take the first bite from the first pizza out of the brand new pizza oven. "Take it from a boy who loves pizza," he would say, "Pizza With a Heart is the best pizza in town." Once in a while, as Lamont bit into the pizza, the image of his mom's chicken pot pie or a bowl of his dad's vegetable soup floated through Lamont's mind.

Using a prediction map

Look back at the prediction you wrote on page 59. Did you predict what would happen next? Now use story clues and what you know to fill in the prediction map below.

Story Clues	What I Already Know

Prediction

60

Read the second part of the realistic fiction story "The Boy Who Loved Pizza."

By the end of the summer, Pizza With a Heart had become the most popular pizza chain in the state. The company invited Lamont and his family to a party to celebrate their success. "Do you think they'll serve pizza?" Lamont asked as they were getting out of the car at company **headquarters**.

"What else would they serve?" his parents and sister said all at once.

None of them heard Lamont's pitiful groan.

When Lamont walked into the party, people cheered and clapped. Mr. Harmony, the president of Pizza With a Heart, invited Lamont on stage to share a piece of pizza with him. Lamont couldn't refuse. He forced himself to smile as he took a bite of pizza. One more time, he repeated his famous line. "Take it from me, the boy who loves pizza, Pizza With a Heart is the best pizza in town."

A little while later, Mrs. Carver took Lamont aside. "Is something wrong, Lamont?" she asked. "You don't look too happy for someone who's going to be a national star."

"I'm sick of pizza," he blurted out. "I don't ever want to eat pizza again in my whole entire life. I'm supposed to be the boy who loves pizza. But now I hate it! And I miss my friends, too. I don't want to be a national star!"

"We thought you were having fun," Mrs. Carver said gently. "If you're not, then you don't have to do this anymore. The contract that we signed with the company **expires** next week. After that, you never ever have to eat pizza again!"

"Never! Really? Thanks, Mom!" he said hugging her. Just then, a waiter with a tray of hot pizza walked by. For a moment, a familiar feeling came over Lamont. "Mom," he said, eyeing the pizza, "exactly how long is *never*?"

Using a prediction map

Look back at the prediction you wrote on page 60. Did you predict what would happen? Now write what happened in the second part of the realistic fiction story.

_____

_____

_____

_____

_____

Check Your Understanding

Think about what you've read. Then answer these questions.

1. Which of these does not help show that Lamont was an ordinary child?
   - Ⓐ He often bumps into people.
   - Ⓑ He argues with his sister Flo.
   - Ⓒ He plays soccer and baseball.
   - Ⓓ He likes pizza more than ice cream, cake, and anything else.

2. Which of these is a story clue that you could have used to predict that Mr. and Mrs. Lamont would call Ms. Santoro?
   - Ⓐ Lamont's parents insist that he eat a balanced diet.
   - Ⓑ Flo sees an ad in the paper.
   - Ⓒ Lamont reads the ad aloud.
   - Ⓓ Flo points out the part of the ad about earning money for college.

3. The ad said that the job would not interfere with school. The job would not
   - Ⓐ get in the way of going to school.
   - Ⓑ require changing schools.
   - Ⓒ take the place of school.
   - Ⓓ start until school was over.

4. In the story, the phrase *here's the deal* means
   - Ⓐ "here are the cards."
   - Ⓑ "this is the business arrangement."
   - Ⓒ "these are the facts."
   - Ⓓ "here is what the dealer thinks."

5. Which of these is a fact from the story?
   - Ⓐ A lot of people like pizza.
   - Ⓑ Most youngsters would choose pizza over Brussels sprouts any day.
   - Ⓒ Mr. and Mrs. Carver agreed to call Ms. Santoro for more information.
   - Ⓓ Whoever gets this job could be a national star!

6. In the story, the meaning of the word *chain* is
   - Ⓐ "a length of metal links."
   - Ⓑ "a number of stores run by one company."
   - Ⓒ "a series of events."
   - Ⓓ "to fasten to something with metal links."

7. What is an example of a commitment?
   - Ⓐ an agreement to help a friend
   - Ⓑ a newspaper advertisement
   - Ⓒ a favorite kind of food, like pizza
   - Ⓓ a child star

8. Which of these is not one of the reasons Ms. Carver offers Lamont the job?
   - Ⓐ He looks good on camera.
   - Ⓑ He is between the ages of 10 and 14.
   - Ⓒ His friends call him "pizza boy."
   - Ⓓ He acts naturally.

9. From the information in the story, you can draw the conclusion that Lamont's parents
   - Ⓐ want Lamont to be a star.
   - Ⓑ let their children do whatever they want as long as they do well in school.
   - Ⓒ eat a lot of pizza.
   - Ⓓ put their children's health and happiness before anything else.

10. When a business agreement expires, it
    - Ⓐ is no longer in effect.
    - Ⓑ is signed.
    - Ⓒ is discussed by a group of people.
    - Ⓓ mysteriously disappears.

11. From the story clues and what you know about how people act in real life, you can predict that

Ⓐ Lamont will become the biggest child star of all time.

Ⓑ Lamont will probably eat pizza again sometime in the future.

Ⓒ Lamont will never have enough money to go to college.

Ⓓ Lamont will miss going to the opening of new Pizza With a Heart stores.

12. The author wrote this story to

Ⓐ tell an entertaining story about a boy who loves pizza.

Ⓑ describe the life of a child star.

Ⓒ explain how to become a spokesperson for a large pizza company.

Ⓓ persuade readers not to eat pizza.

Extend Your Learning

- *Write a New Story Ending*

  In small groups, brainstorm ideas for a new story ending for "The Boy Who Loved Pizza." You might start by imagining what might happen if Lamont changes his mind and decides that he wants to be a national star. Use a prediction map to predict the kinds of things that might happen as a result. How would his life change? Where might he have to go? What might he have to do? Whom might he meet? Answer these and other questions of your own as you complete the prediction map. Then use your predictions to write a new story ending. Share your new ending with the class.

- *Find Facts About Pizza*

  Reread the Prepare for the Reading Selection passage on page 57. Then use the Internet and other resources to gather more information about pizza. Look for facts and details about the history of pizza and the different kinds of pizza. Learn about pizza's nutritional value. Then do a quick survey among classmates to find out their favorite pizza toppings. Share what you learn in a written or oral report, or in a poster.

- *Read a Realistic Fiction Story*

  Read with a partner another realistic fiction story of your choice. As you read, stop every once in a while to each make predictions about what will happen next. Use story clues and what you know to make predictions. Record your predictions in a prediction map. Continue to read to check your predictions and make new ones.

LESSON 7 Finding Word Meaning in Context

Learn About Finding Word Meaning in Context

Thinking about the strategy

When you read, you may encounter new or unfamiliar words. Often, you can use **context clues** to figure out the meaning of these words. Context clues usually appear in the words, phrases, and sentences that surround the unfamiliar word. This chart lists different types of context clues that you can use to figure out a word's meaning.

Context Clues	Examples
Synonym (a word that means the same)	Connie's **glum** expression mirrored her *gloomy* mood.
Antonym (a word that means the opposite)	The house had a **sinister** quality, but its owners appeared *good* and kind.
Definition	An **excerpt** is a *short section that is taken from a longer piece of writing*.
Restatement	The **exterior**, or *outside*, of the home had signs of decay.
Examples	A **catastrophe**, such as an *earthquake* or a *flood*, can cause widespread destruction.

Good readers often combine context clues and a sense of what they are reading to find the meaning of a new word. Sometimes, however, the context clues may be weak, or the word may be related to a topic that readers know nothing about. When you cannot be sure of a word's meaning, use a dictionary or a glossary to check the meaning.

Studying a model

Read the passage and the notes beside it.

The word guess *is a context clue to the meaning of* speculate, *which means "to guess."*

The phrase "as if she didn't care" is a context clue to the meaning of nonchalant, *which means "not excited."*

"Usually, I don't like to speculate," the antique dealer said. "But at first glance I'd guess that this silver bowl dates back to the 1700s. The workmanship is exquisite. I've never seen anything quite like it. I'd have to examine it more closely, of course, but it's probably worth about $50,000."

The woman tried to act nonchalant. "That's very interesting," she said coolly, as if she didn't care. "I recognized its beauty myself, but I didn't realize it was so old."

Learn About a Graphic Organizer

Understanding a words-and-meaning chart

A **words-and-meaning chart** will help you identify unknown words and the context clues that you can use to figure out the meaning of these words. When you are reading for enjoyment, you may wish to jot down unknown words in the chart and the pages where they appear. Then you can go back to identify context clues that will help you understand the meaning of these words. When you are reading to understand, you can use the chart to determine a word's meaning before reading on in the text.

Here is a words-and-meaning chart for the passage on page 64. It shows context clues and what the reader thinks each word means, based on the context clues.

Find clues to a word's meaning in surrounding words and sentences and list them here.
▼

List new or unknown words here. ▶

Word	Context Clues	What I Think Word Means
speculate	I'd guess; it's probably worth about $50,000	to guess
exquisite	I've never seen anything quite like it; its beauty	extremely beautiful
nonchalant	tried to act; she said coolly, as if she didn't care	acting cool; not excited

◀ *Write what you think the word means based on all the clues you use.*

When you complete a words-and-meaning chart, you use context clues to determine the meaning of an unknown word. You get a clearer understanding of what a sentence, paragraph, or selection is about.

Why does the woman act nonchalant when she hears what the bowl is worth? She may be worried that if the dealer realizes how excited and needy she really is, he may offer her less than the bowl is worth.

As you read, ask yourself

- How is the unknown word used in the sentence? How does it relate to the sense of the whole passage?
- What words surrounding the unknown word provide clues to its meaning?
- Where can I look to check the meaning of the unknown word?

Learn About a Form of Writing

Focusing on
an interview

An **interview** is a series of questions and answers, usually between a reporter and a well-known person. The person may be well-known to people in a community, the country, or the entire world. Interview questions are usually designed to highlight the important details and accomplishments in the life of the person being interviewed.

An interview often has these elements.

- It contains a series of questions and answers.

- Its main purpose is to reveal interesting facts and details about the person being interviewed.

- It offers the person being interviewed a chance to give his or her opinions on a topic.

Here is a part of an interview between a newspaper reporter and a fifth-grade boy who started his own business.

> **The *Sun* Reporter:**   Jamie, you are quite an enterprising young man. There aren't too many other fifth graders who have the energy and daring to start their own businesses. What makes you so unique?
>
> **Jamie Edwards:**   I don't think I'm that different from other children my age. However, I do have a lot of enthusiasm, or eagerness, to succeed. I think that's really important because running a business is a challenge.

Organizing ideas in
a words-and-meaning
chart

You can use a words-and-meaning chart to determine the meaning of unknown words in an interview. Understanding the meaning of these words will help you understand the responses the person being interviewed gives and make the interview more interesting. Here is a filled-in words-and-meaning chart for the interview above.

Word	Context Clues	What I Think Word Means
enterprising	energy, daring, start own business	being willing and having the energy to try something new or different
unique	there aren't too many other; different	one of a kind; the only one
enthusiasm	eagerness	lively interest

Prepare for the Reading Selection

Gaining knowledge

When Maurice Sendak was a young boy in Brooklyn, New York, his family moved so frequently that he never had a chance to make friends. He was also a sickly child who watched from his bedroom window as other children played outside. To keep busy and take his mind off his misery, Sendak would draw the people and the places in his neighborhood. Then he would make up fantastic stories to go with them. Sendak, of course, grew up to become one of the most popular authors and illustrators of children's books of all time. *Where the Wild Things Are*, Sendak's most famous work, was published in 1963.

The interview with Maurice Sendak, which you will read on the pages that follow, is from a series of on-line interviews with well-known authors. Each of the authors was asked what books he or she thought every child should read.

Learn Vocabulary

Understanding vocabulary

The boxed words below are **boldfaced** in the selection. Learn the meaning of each word. Then write the word that could replace the underlined word or words in the sentence.

| incredible |
| unwittingly |
| gruesome |
| hilarious |
| consisted |
| binding |
| demise |

1. The book has a leather <u>cover that holds the pages together</u>.

   _____

2. Your story about the bear and the campers was <u>unbelievable</u>.

   _____

3. My brother told us that <u>frightening and horrible</u> tale just to scare us.

   _____

4. Dinner <u>was made up</u> of a bowl of soup and a few crackers.

   _____

5. She left the cage door open <u>without meaning to</u>, and the snake

   crawled out. _____

6. This book ends with the <u>death</u> of the old goldfish.

   _____

7. The joke that José told was <u>very, very funny</u>. _____

Read the first part of "An Interview With Maurice Sendak." This interview is excerpted from "Maurice Sendak: A Western Canon, Jr." by Marion Long.

An Interview With Maurice Sendak

HOMEARTS: What person deserves greatest credit for your love of reading?

SENDAK: My father. He was an **incredible** storyteller. He told stories to put us to sleep at night, my brother and sister and me. Which was wonderful, although—**unwittingly**, of course—he did turn me into an insomniac, because some of his stories were so hair-raising. And he didn't edit.

It's funny, because that's what I'm accused of now: being a storyteller who tells children inappropriate things. And I must have learned it at his knee, because he never thought that any story was inappropriate for kids—if it was a good story. So he was the perfect children's writer, in my opinion, because he told us what we really wanted to hear—all the details—sometimes **gruesome**, sometimes **hilarious**, and sometimes bewildering because we didn't understand everything. Or at least I didn't: I was the youngest. My sister was almost ten years older than me, my brother five, and I was very jealous of the fact that they read real books. And so I only wanted to read their books.

HOMEARTS: What were some of the books that were most important to you as a child?

SENDAK: To have become a reader was faintly miraculous for me, given how nightmarish reading was made for us in school. I have the most intense memory of what reading meant: You went to assembly and you sat, row by row, class by class. And then a teacher on stage read the story. Reading **consisted** of listening with your hands folded in your lap. Kids assigned by teachers to be monitors walked up and down to see if your hands indeed were clasped tightly. If your hands were folded during the entire reading, you might get a tiny gold star, which you would paste in your book. So of course all you thought about were your hands. I dreaded it, but we had to endure. And you see how anti-reading, how anti-life, the situation was.

There are very few books from school that I loved. In fact, there's only one—*Chicken Little*. And I remember it not because *Chicken Little* is such a great story, but because of the pictures. It was a school reader, and the pictures were simple and they were all yellow. And I loved to turn the page and see all those yellow pictures: little, fat, yellow pictures running all over the pages.

The other book that meant an awful lot to me was . . .
A Child's Garden of Verses by Robert Louis Stevenson. That
has very happy associations for me because I was an extremely
sickly child, which was fairly normal back in the 30's before
sulfa drugs and so on. Kids caught everything back then: the
whooping cough, scarlet fever, all of that. I got everything and
spent a good part of my early years in bed. And *A Child's
Garden of Verses* was read to me by my brother. Some of the
poems I memorized. I remember one in particular about the
counterpane, with soldiers on the blanket ["The Land of
Counterpane"] because that was what my life was like.

Completing a words-and-meaning chart

Some of the words-and-meaning chart for the first part of the interview
has been filled in. Complete the chart with more words that are new or
unknown to you.

Word	Context Clues	What I Think Word Means
insomniac	told stories to put us to sleep; he did turn me into . . . ; some of his stories were hair-raising	someone who can't fall asleep
edit	he didn't edit; he told us what we really wanted to hear	take out or change parts of a story or written work

Reading Selection—Part Two

Read the second part of "An Interview With Maurice Sendak."

HOMEARTS: What were some of the books that were most important to you as a child? *(continued)*

The first real book I ever owned was *The Prince and the Pauper* by Mark Twain, which my sister bought me. And I flipped when she did. I still have it—that poor, abused book. I smelled it, I squeezed it, I tried to bite into it. I couldn't believe that I had such a book, that I owned such a rare thing. Beautiful red cloth, a shiny picture pasted on the **binding**, and beautiful end-papers. It stood on my dresser, it came to bed with me, I stroked it. I didn't actually read it until many years later. And I like *The Prince and the Pauper*, but first and foremost was the joy of the object itself.

HOMEARTS: What books would be in your Western Canon for children?

SENDAK: *A Child's Garden of Verses*, certainly, and some of Mark Twain's novels, for starters. My first major step into literature occurred when my father joined a book club and we got a set of Mark Twain. The volumes had beautiful green bindings, and on each spine was a black square, inside of which was a stamped gold coinlike profile of Mark Twain, which you could feel with your fingers. And as you can imagine, there was a lot of fingering going on when I got my hands on those books.

Tom Sawyer was the beginning of literature for me. I just loved it. And later, *Huckleberry Finn*, which I loved even more. Of course, *The Prince and the Pauper* had preceded them, but that had more to do with the externals of the book.

Another work in my Canon would be a short story by Bret Harte that I fell in love with very early on: "The Luck of Roaring Camp." I even did illustrations for it. I must have been about eleven or twelve when I did my first pictures for a book, and I chose "The Luck of Roaring Camp." I still have my old and only edition. I recollect that the story had to do with a baby and a rough mining camp, and, I believe, the sad **demise** of the baby. It was already my interest in children, my interest in babies, even when I was still a child myself, that led me to that story.

HOMEARTS: What do you think parents need to do, or what can parents do, to help their children become readers?

SENDAK: I think it's an easy physical thing: When my father read to me, I leaned into him so I became part of his chest or his forearm. And I think children who are hugged, and children who are held on laps . . . will always associate reading with the bodies of their parents, the smells of their parents. And that will always keep you a reader. Because that perfume, that sensuous connection is lifelong.

Using a words-and-meaning chart

Fill in the words-and-meaning chart to find the meaning of new or unknown words in the second part of the interview.

Word	Context Clues	What I Think Word Means

Check Your Understanding

Think about what you've read. Then answer these questions.

1. Whom does Maurice Sendak say was responsible for his love of reading?
   - Ⓐ his father
   - Ⓑ his sister
   - Ⓒ his brother
   - Ⓓ his teacher

2. If someone tells you an incredible story, you will probably
   - Ⓐ start to cry.
   - Ⓑ laugh for a very long time.
   - Ⓒ become quite frightened.
   - Ⓓ find the story hard to believe.

3. Which word is a synonym for *unwittingly*?
   - Ⓐ seriously
   - Ⓑ accidentally
   - Ⓒ wisely
   - Ⓓ softly

4. From what Sendak says, you can draw the conclusion that his idea of a good story is
   - Ⓐ one that is not suitable for small children.
   - Ⓑ one that could never happen.
   - Ⓒ one with lots of colorful, exciting details.
   - Ⓓ one with pictures.

5. In Part One, the best meaning of the word *assembly* is
   - Ⓐ "the library."
   - Ⓑ "a group gathering."
   - Ⓒ "a place for disobedient children."
   - Ⓓ "an imaginary place."

6. Which of these explains the difference between how Sendak learned to read and how most children learn to read?
   - Ⓐ He listened to books being read instead of reading them.
   - Ⓑ He had to read with his hands in his lap.
   - Ⓒ He was not allowed to read until he was ten.
   - Ⓓ He had to read aloud on stage in front of all the children in the school.

7. In Part One, which clue word is a synonym for *counterpane*?
   - Ⓐ soldiers
   - Ⓑ life
   - Ⓒ bed
   - Ⓓ blanket

8. In Part Two, when Sendak says "I flipped," he means that he
   - Ⓐ did somersaults.
   - Ⓑ opened the cover of a book.
   - Ⓒ became excited and happy.
   - Ⓓ fell down.

9. Where would you expect to see a binding?
   - Ⓐ on a bed
   - Ⓑ on a face
   - Ⓒ on a coin
   - Ⓓ on a book

10. *The Prince and the Pauper* was special to Sendak mainly because
    - Ⓐ it was the beginning of literature for him.
    - Ⓑ he loved the physical beauty of the book.
    - Ⓒ he did illustrations for it.
    - Ⓓ his sister gave it to him.

11. Which of these books does Sendak name first for his Western Canon for children?

Ⓐ *A Child's Garden of Verses*

Ⓑ *The Prince and the Pauper*

Ⓒ *Chicken Little*

Ⓓ *Huckleberry Finn*

12. Sendak believes that children will become lifelong readers if

Ⓐ parents order beautiful sets of books from book clubs.

Ⓑ children sit quietly and listen to their parents read to them.

Ⓒ parents hold children close when reading to them.

Ⓓ children have a chance to illustrate their favorite stories.

Extend Your Learning

• *Write an Interview*

Use the questions from "An Interview With Maurice Sendak," or write your own questions to interview a classmate about his or her interest in books and reading. Write the questions on a piece of paper, leaving enough space to write responses. As you conduct the interview, be polite, and be sure that you record your classmate's responses accurately and as completely as possible. If your classmate does not object, you may wish to submit a final copy of the interview to the school or local paper.

• *Read an Interview*

Locate and read an interview with a popular or favorite children's author. You might begin by looking at the web sites of publishers of children's books. As you read the interview, use a words-and-meaning chart to list unknown words and to figure out their meanings. After reading, share in a small group what you learn about the author.

• *Compile a List of Favorite Books*

List three of your favorite books and make notes about why they are your favorites. Then with your class, create a Top Ten Book List. Be prepared to support your choices and to state why you think each of the books you have listed should make the Top Ten List. After everyone has presented his or her choices, decide together which books should be on the final list. Next to each title on the list, write the author and a brief explanation of why the book is worth reading. Post the list in the school library.

LESSON 8 Drawing Conclusions and Making Inferences

Learn About Drawing Conclusions and Making Inferences

Thinking about the strategy

When you read, you may discover that the author has left out details about the characters, setting, and events in a story. As a good reader, you can combine the details that the author does provide and what you know from personal experience and knowledge to **draw conclusions** or **make inferences**.

Identify story clues.	Use prior knowledge.

Draw a conclusion or make an inference.

A logical conclusion or inference makes sense, based on information in the story and what you know from personal experience. You cannot draw a logical conclusion or make a logical inference without enough information or without the correct information. If you do not have enough information or if you use the wrong information, your conclusions or inferences may be wrong.

Studying a model

Read the story and the notes beside it.

The author gives these details: Liana spends hours outdoors; says "There's always so much going on"; she observed.

You know that people who spend a lot of time doing something are often fascinated by it.

One conclusion you can draw is that Liana is fascinated by nature.

Everyone said that Liana didn't know how to be bored. On beautiful sunny summer days, she spent hours outdoors. "There's always so much going on," she told her friends who couldn't understand how she could just sit on the grass, doing nothing. But Liana didn't just sit. She observed. She watched the robins as they gathered leaves and tiny twigs to build their nest. She watched bees, flit from flower to flower, collecting nectar to make honey. She watched as inchworms arched their backs and then dragged their bodies forward to crawl.

Later, back in her room, Liana drew beautiful, detailed drawings of all she had observed. Several of Liana's drawings had won prizes in art competitions.

Learn About a Graphic Organizer

Understanding a conclusions/inferences diagram

A **conclusions/inferences diagram** can help you identify the details that you need to draw conclusions or make inferences about the characters, setting, and events in a story. You can use a conclusions/inferences diagram when reading a variety of fiction and nonfiction works, including short stories, fables, articles, and biographies.

Here is a conclusions/inferences diagram for the story on page 74.

List details about characters, setting, and events that the author gives.

What the Author Tells Me	What I Know
Liana spends hours outdoors. Her friends don't understand. She observes things in nature closely. Her drawings have won prizes.	People who spend a lot of time outdoors are usually nature lovers. Friends who do not understand one's interests usually have different interests. People closely observe what interests them. Talented artists win art contests.

List what you know about people, places, and events from your own experience.

Draw conclusions that make sense based on what the author tells you and what you know.

What I Can Figure Out

Liana is probably a nature lover, who is fascinated by even the smallest details in nature.

Liana is probably more interested in nature than her friends are, and more knowledgeable.

Liana is a talented artist.

When you complete a conclusions/inferences diagram, you figure out ideas that are not clearly or completely explained in a selection.

Why does Liana spend hours observing nature?
She is fascinated by nature and interested in learning as much as she can through observation.

As you read, ask yourself

- What details does the author provide about characters, setting, or events?
- What do I know from personal experience about people, places, and events?
- What conclusions make sense, based on what the author tells me and what I already know?

Learn About a Form of Writing

A **biography** is the true story of a person's life told by another person. The author of a biography is called the biographer. A biographer uses facts and details that illustrate why the person's life is important and why it is of interest to others. A biography usually covers a person's entire life. If the person is important because of one special accomplishment, the biographer may focus on that part of the person's life.

A biography has these features.

- It tells important dates, places, and events in the person's life.
- It is written from the author's point of view.
- It explains why the person's life is important.

Here is a paragraph from a biography about Elizabeth Blackwell.

> In 1832, no woman had ever been admitted into a medical school. While most ordinary girls in America would not have dreamed of being doctors, young Elizabeth Blackwell dreamt of nothing else. The twelve-year-old, whose family had recently moved to New York City from England, was determined to be a doctor. Nothing was going to stop her.

Organizing ideas in a conclusions/inferences diagram

A biographer may not tell you every detail about a person's life. You can use a conclusions/inferences diagram to figure out things the author does not completely explain. Here is a filled-in conclusions/inferences diagram for the paragraph above.

What the Author Tells Me	What I Know
No woman had ever been admitted to medical school.	Doctors attend medical school.
Most ordinary girls would not dream of becoming doctors; Elizabeth did.	Extraordinary people do things that ordinary people don't.

What I Can Figure Out
There were no female doctors when Elizabeth Blackwell was a child.
Elizabeth Blackwell was an extraordinary young girl.

Prepare for the Reading Selection

Gaining knowledge

The United States of America was still a young, struggling nation when Congress declared war against Great Britain on June 18, 1812. Americans had not forgotten the Revolution and their battle for independence from England. As a result, many Americans still harbored ill-will against the British. These negative feelings increased when Great Britain interfered with American shipping and began forcing captured American sailors to serve on British ships. On the pages that follow, you will read a biography. By the time the events described in the biography took place, America and Great Britain had been at war for two years.

Learn Vocabulary

Understanding vocabulary

The boxed words below are **boldfaced** in the selection. Learn the meaning of each word. Then write the word beside its definition.

remnant
assault
anthem
obscurity
intervened
sloop
detained
barriers
commissioned
distributed

1. came between to change the outcome _____

2. a violent attack _____

3. a small sailing vessel _____

4. a patriotic song _____

5. something left over _____

6. handed out _____

7. things that are in the way _____

8. hired to perform a specific task _____

9. without fame _____

10. held under guard, as in jail _____

Read the first part of the biography "Francis Scott Key and a Nation's Banner."

Francis Scott Key and a Nation's Banner

Each day, for a few moments at a time, visitors to the Smithsonian's Museum of American History in Washington, D.C., glimpse the fragile **remnant** of a flag in dim light behind a glass wall. It is a flag that symbolizes America's determination to be an independent nation. It is the flag that flew high above brave, battle-weary Americans who had endured a 25-hour **assault** by British troops at Fort McHenry during the War of 1812. It is a flag that inspired a young lawyer to write a poem that more than one hundred years later would become our country's national **anthem**. It is the flag known as the Star Spangled Banner. The young lawyer and amateur poet who honored that flag in verse was Francis Scott Key.

Francis Scott Key was born on August 1, 1779, on his family's Maryland estate, Terra Rubra. The son of a Revolutionary officer, Key received his early elementary school education at home. At the age of 10, he left home to attend private school in Annapolis, Maryland. He later graduated from St. John's College, and soon after began to practice law. In 1802, he moved to Georgetown, near the nation's capital, and opened a successful law practice. As a hobby, Key enjoyed writing poetry.

Except for a series of events, Key might have lived and died in **obscurity**. However, fate **intervened**, and Key became an eyewitness to one of America's proudest moments. As a result, the name of Francis Scott Key will forever be linked with the story of America and her flag.

In 1812, war broke out between Great Britain and a young American nation. The British fleet sailed into Chesapeake Bay on August 19, 1814. Within five days, British troops had captured Washington and burned the White House and the Capitol building. By then President James Madison, his wife, and other important officials were safely away.

Once the capital was defeated, British troops returned to their ships and prepared to attack Baltimore. Among their prisoners was an elderly physician named Dr. William Beanes. He had been captured while tending to British soldiers, injured during the battle to capture Washington.

Beanes and Key were good friends. When Key heard that his friend had been captured, he asked President Madison for permission to seek the release of Beanes. Madison agreed and sent Colonel John Skinner to accompany Key.

On September 5, 1814, Key and Skinner sailed to the British ship the *Tonnant*, where Beanes was being kept. At first, British officers were reluctant to let Beanes go. Then Key showed them letters that wounded British soldiers had written, praising Dr. Beanes. The officers decided to set Beanes free.

Although the British officers agreed to let Beanes go, they felt that Key, Skinner, and Beanes knew too much about the British plan to attack Baltimore. Therefore, the three men could not be released until after the battle. The three Americans were transported to another British ship, and then back to their own **sloop**. There they were **detained** under British guard.

Completing a conclusions/inferences diagram

Some of the conclusions/inferences diagram has been filled in. Add more details from the first part of the biography.

What the Author Tells Me	What I Know
A fragile remnant of the flag is displayed in low light behind glass at the Smithsonian.	Dust and light can damage cloth over time.

What I Can Figure Out

The flag that flew over Fort McHenry has become fragile, or delicate, over time.
By keeping it out of the light, the Smithsonian is trying to protect it from further damage.

Read the second part of the biography "Francis Scott Key and a Nation's Banner."

While the British fleet moved closer to Baltimore, an inexperienced American militia under the command of Major George Armistead prepared for battle. **Barriers** were erected around the city of Baltimore, and a brand new American flag flapped in the wind over Fort McHenry.

Several months earlier, Armistead had **commissioned** flagmaker Mary Young Pickersgill to make a flag that the British would be sure to see. Pickersgill, with the help of her daughter Caroline, crafted a flag that measured forty-two feet by thirty feet, and had 15 stars and 15 stripes. Flying boldly above the fort, the flag was visible not only to the approaching British, but also to Key, Skinner, and Beanes, aboard the sloop.

By the morning of September 13, well-trained British troops had gone ashore, and the British fleet launched its attack. All day, the British bombarded Fort McHenry with rockets and bombshells. However, the Americans fought back, and sunk twenty-two British ships.

The sounds of the raging battle kept a glimmer of hope alive in Francis Scott Key and his companions, who had taken refuge in their cabin. As daylight dwindled, Key dared to go on deck. Peering through a haze of smoke, he saw that the flag was still flying. For a while, the battle died down, but around one o'clock in the morning on September 14, as thunder and lightning staged a battle in the sky, the shelling resumed. Once again, Key crept on deck. He was encouraged to see that the flag, although soaked by rain, was still there.

The next morning, an eerie silence filled the air. Key, Skinner, and Beanes could not know it yet, but the British were retreating. The battle and the storm had ended. As the Americans stood on deck of their sloop and gazed toward Fort McHenry, they saw a glorious sight.

Francis Scott Key pulled a letter from his pocket. On the back, he began to compose a poem to celebrate this historic occasion. Later, back in his hotel room, he completed the four-stanza poem, which began with the lines, "O say can you see, by the dawn's early light . . ."

Key's brother-in-law, Judge J.H. Nicholson, encouraged Key to have the poem printed. Copies of the poem, which they titled "Defense of Fort McHenry," were **distributed** around Baltimore. Soon after, the poem appeared in newspapers around the nation with the note that it should be sung to the tune of the song "Anacreon in Heaven." Within months, people all over America were singing Key's song, known by then as "The Star-Spangled Banner."

Following the events at Fort McHenry, Francis Scott Key returned to his law practice in Georgetown, where he lived with his wife Mary and their eleven children. In 1833, President Andrew Jackson appointed Key district attorney for the District of Columbia. Key, who opposed slavery, was also a founder of the American Colonization Society. This group worked to resettle freed slaves in Liberia, on the west coast of Africa.

Francis Scott Key died in 1843. "The Star Spangled Banner" became the official anthem of the United States in 1931.

Using a conclusions/inferences diagram

Use details from the second half of the biography to fill in the conclusions/inferences diagram.

What the Author Tells Me	What I Know

What I Can Figure Out

Check Your Understanding

Think about what you've read. Then answer these questions.

1. Which of these statements about Francis Scott Key is not true?
   - Ⓐ He was born in 1779 in Maryland.
   - Ⓑ He was a lawyer.
   - Ⓒ He was an amateur poet.
   - Ⓓ He was a well-known songwriter.

2. An anthem is something that is
   - Ⓐ sung at national events.
   - Ⓑ eaten on special occasions.
   - Ⓒ presented as a gift.
   - Ⓓ fought over.

3. From the information in Part One of the biography, you can draw the conclusion that Francis Scott Key
   - Ⓐ had many hobbies.
   - Ⓑ was an excellent student.
   - Ⓒ was from a wealthy family.
   - Ⓓ opposed all wars.

4. If Francis Scott Key had lived in obscurity, he would probably have been
   - Ⓐ forgotten.
   - Ⓑ praised.
   - Ⓒ punished.
   - Ⓓ disliked.

5. Which of these events happened last?
   - Ⓐ The British burned Washington.
   - Ⓑ The British attacked Baltimore.
   - Ⓒ President Madison escaped the White House.
   - Ⓓ Francis Scott Key and Colonel Skinner boarded the *Tonnant*.

6. From the details in the biography, you can draw the conclusion that Dr. Beanes was
   - Ⓐ a troublemaker.
   - Ⓑ sickly.
   - Ⓒ a spy.
   - Ⓓ caring.

7. What finally convinced the British officers to release Dr. Beanes?
   - Ⓐ a special request from President James Madison
   - Ⓑ the sight of the American flag
   - Ⓒ letters from wounded British soldiers
   - Ⓓ a poem written by Francis Scott Key

8. Which of these statements is an opinion?
   - Ⓐ The American militia was not very experienced.
   - Ⓑ Major George Armistead commanded the American militia.
   - Ⓒ Mary Young Pickersgill made the flag with her daughter's help.
   - Ⓓ The flag had 15 stars and 15 stripes.

9. In Part Two, the word *bombarded* means
   - Ⓐ "defeated in battle."
   - Ⓑ "watched over."
   - Ⓒ "attacked with explosives."
   - Ⓓ "sneaked up on."

10. Which of these gives human traits to an event of nature?
    - Ⓐ A brand new American flag flapped in the wind.
    - Ⓑ Thunder and lightning staged a battle in the sky.
    - Ⓒ Daylight dwindled.
    - Ⓓ Francis Scott Key crept on deck.

11. Which of these details does not belong in a summary of the biography?
   Ⓐ Francis Scott Key received his early education at home.
   Ⓑ Francis Scott Key's friend, Dr. William Beanes, was captured by the British.
   Ⓒ Francis Scott Key boarded a British ship to seek the release of Dr. Beanes.
   Ⓓ When Francis Scott Key saw that the flag was still flying above Fort McHenry, he began to write a poem.

12. The author wrote this biography mainly to
   Ⓐ describe how the flag called the Star Spangled Banner was made.
   Ⓑ explain how Francis Scott Key came to write "The Star Spangled Banner."
   Ⓒ tell a story about a doctor captured during the War of 1812.
   Ⓓ convince readers to visit the Smithsonian to see the Star Spangled Banner.

Extend Your Learning

- *Write a Biography*

   Write a short biography of someone from American history. Choose a person that you know something about and would like to learn more about. Use library resources and the Internet to read about this person. As you read, fill in a conclusions/inferences diagram. When you write your biography, try to include facts and conclusions from your diagram. Share your biography with classmates.

- *Research the Flag*

   Do research to learn more about the history of the American flag. Jot down facts and details in a chart, web, or other graphic organizer. Then use the information that you gather to make a poster about the American flag. Display the poster in the classroom or school library.

- *Listen to Patriotic Music*

   As a group, listen to recordings of "The Star Spangled Banner" and other popular American patriotic songs, such as "America the Beautiful" and "My Country 'Tis of Thee." As you listen, consider whether you think that "The Star Spangled Banner" is the best choice for our national anthem, or if one of the other songs should be our anthem. Discuss and debate your ideas in small groups. Share the results of your discussion with the whole class.

Distinguishing Between Fact and Opinion

Learn About Distinguishing Between Fact and Opinion

Thinking about the strategy

When you read an informational article, essay, or other nonfiction work, you learn facts about a topic. At the same time, you are also likely to discover the author's opinions on the topic. Being able to distinguish between facts and opinions as you read can help you understand what an author is trying to accomplish.

A **fact** is a statement that contains information that can be proved, checked, or tested. An **opinion** is a statement that cannot be proved. An opinion expresses an author's belief, thought, or feeling.

To prove, check, or test a fact	• Look in a reliable source, such as an encyclopedia or a textbook. • Look at a reliable Internet site. • Ask an expert on the topic. • Use your own knowledge and experience.
To identify an opinion	• Look for a statement that expresses a personal belief, thought, or feeling. • Look for words that signal opinions, such as *I feel*, *I think*, and *in my opinion*. • Look for words that describe and qualify, such as *greatest*, *best*, *always*, *never*, *most*, and *least*.

You may discover that a statement is inaccurate or false. Then the statement is neither a fact nor an opinion. It is just an incorrect statement.

Studying a model

Read the opening paragraph from a book report and the notes beside it.

The statement about the title and author is a fact.

The details that tell what the story is about can be checked.

The words interesting, heartwarming, and in my opinion signal statements of opinion.

A Family Apart by Joan Lowery Nixon takes place in 1860. The book tells what happens to six children when their mother, who cannot take care of them, puts them on the "orphan train" and sends them from New York to Missouri. This is an interesting and heartwarming story. The train journey west is long and sometimes boring. However, several events occur that add excitement to the trip. In my opinion, the most exciting moment is when outlaws rob the train.

Learn About a Graphic Organizer

Understanding a fact-and-opinion chart

A **fact-and-opinion chart** will help you distinguish between facts and opinions when you read. You can use a fact-and-opinion chart to identify facts and opinions in letters to the editor, essays, articles, and other nonfiction and fiction works.

Here is a fact-and-opinion chart for the opening paragraph from a book report on page 84. It shows statements in the paragraph that are facts and statements that express the author's opinions.

FACT *Can it be proved, checked, or tested?* *Is it something someone knows from experience?*	OPINION *Is it what someone believes, thinks, or feels?*
A Family Apart was written by Joan Lowery Nixon. *The story takes place in 1860.* *The story tells what happens to six children after their mother puts them on an "orphan train" to Missouri.*	*This is an interesting and heartwarming story.* *The train journey west is long and sometimes boring.* *Several events occur that add excitement to the trip.* *In my opinion, the most exciting moment is when outlaws rob the train.*

In this column, list statements that contain information that can be proved, checked, or tested through a reliable or expert source.

In this column, list statements that express an author's or a character's beliefs, thoughts, or feelings.

When you complete a fact-and-opinion chart, you distinguish between facts and opinions. This can help you evaluate what you are reading to better understand what an author is trying to do.

What does the author want me to believe about the book A Family Apart? It is an interesting and exciting story that is worth reading.

As you read, ask yourself

- Can the information in this statement be proved, checked, or tested?
- Does this statement express a belief, thought, or feeling?
- Are there words or phrases that signal an opinion?

Learn About a Form of Writing

Focusing on a letter to the editor

Many newspapers and magazines print **letters to the editor** that have been sent in by readers. A letter to the editor often contains a writer's personal opinions about a current event or an issue of interest to the community.

A letter to the editor often has these features.

- It expresses a writer's opinion.
- It contains facts and details that support the writer's opinion.
- It may ask readers to do something or to believe something.
- It follows business letter form.

Here is a letter to the editor of a newspaper. As you read, think about what the writer wants readers to believe or to do.

> Dear Editor:
>
> In last week's paper, you printed a letter from Ali Turner. Ali wrote to complain about the new Axis Mall policy. This policy forbids large groups of young people from hanging around the mall. In my opinion, the new policy is a good thing. Girls and boys my age should be able to find better things to do than walk up and down the length of a mall. I think that parents and their children should support the new policy.
>
> Yours truly,
> Carlos Lopez

Organizing ideas in a fact-and-opinion chart

You can use a fact-and-opinion chart when reading letters to the editor. Here is a filled-in fact-and-opinion chart for the letter above.

FACT *Can it be proved, checked, or tested? Is it something someone knows from experience?*	OPINION *Is it what someone believes, thinks, or feels?*
The paper printed a letter from Ali Turner. Ali wrote to complain about the new mall policy. The policy forbids large groups of young people from hanging around the mall.	In my opinion, the new policy is a good thing. Girls and boys my age should be able to find better things to do. I think parents and children should support the policy.

Prepare for the Reading Selection

Gaining knowledge

The letters to the editor that you will read on the following pages focus on skateboarding and on public attitudes toward skateboarders. The sport of skateboarding began in California when a group of ocean surfers were looking for a way to surf when there were no waves. At first, skateboarding was mostly a sport for teenaged boys. In more recent years, younger boys and girls have become involved with the sport, both as skaters and as fans at skateboarding competitions. Through the years, the biggest obstacle skateboarders have faced is where to practice tricks and moves safely, without annoying the general public. In the 1970s, some cities built skate parks, but high insurance costs and the threat of lawsuits forced them to close. Today, however, adults recognize the need to provide skateboarders with a safe place to practice their sport. As a result, more and more cities and towns across the country are setting aside specific areas for skateboarders, or are building well-equipped skateboard parks.

Learn Vocabulary

Understanding vocabulary

The boxed words below are **boldfaced** in the selection. Learn the meaning of each word. Then write the word whose meaning is similar to the given word.

| hoodlums |
| incident |
| pedestrians |
| petition |
| ban |
| trend |
| site |

1. walkers _____

2. location _____

3. event _____

4. request _____

5. forbid _____

6. outlaws _____

7. direction _____

Read the first letter to the editor.

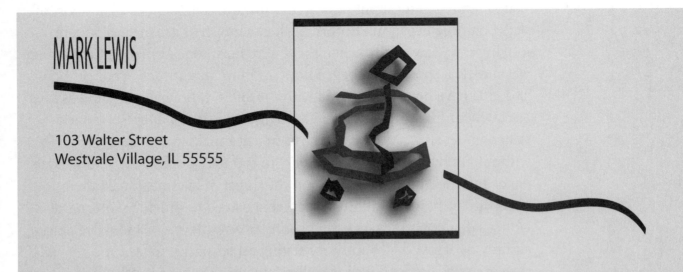

MARK LEWIS

103 Walter Street
Westvale Village, IL 55555

April 12, 2001

Letters to the Editor
The Sentinel
500 Main Drive
Westvale Village, IL 55555

Dear Editor:

 I am a skateboarder. I started skateboarding when I was in the third grade. My older brothers taught me basic tricks. Then, last year, when I was in fourth grade, I signed up for skateboarding lessons. I learned new moves that made skateboarding even more fun. I also learned how important it is to wear safety gear and to obey the safety rules. I love skateboarding. In my opinion, it's an exciting, thrilling sport that requires concentration, talent, and skill.

 Some people in our community believe that all skateboarders are **hoodlums** who have no manners or concern for others. The recent **incident** in the park between a skateboarder and two joggers has once again cast a dark shadow upon skateboarders. In my opinion, it's totally unfair to label all skateboarders as inconsiderate just because of the actions of one thoughtless skateboarder.

 Last year, the Park Commission passed a bill. This bill allows skateboarders to use the Center Hill area of the park on Mondays through Fridays, from 4 P.M. to 6 P.M.; and on Saturdays and Sundays, from noon to 4 P.M. All the skateboarders I know appreciate having a place to skateboard. We are all careful to follow the rules that are posted in the park.

Most people believe that it makes sense for skateboarders to use the park. However, some **pedestrians** and joggers object. They have signed a **petition** to **ban** all skateboarders from the park. This action is unfair. If skateboarders are banned from the park, where are they supposed to go? Skateboarding in the street is against the law. It's too dangerous anyway.

Skateboarding is a sport, just like baseball, softball, and soccer. The Park Commission provides park fields for all these sports. Skateboarders have just as much right to use the park as baseball players, softball players, and soccer players.

Sincerely,

Mark Lewis

Mark Lewis

Completing a fact-and-opinion chart

Some of the fact-and-opinion chart has been filled in. Add more facts and opinions from the first letter to the editor.

FACT Can it be proved, checked, or tested? Is it something someone knows from experience?	OPINION Is it what someone believes, thinks, or feels?
I am a skateboarder. I started skateboarding in third grade.	I love skateboarding. In my opinion, it's an exciting, thrilling sport.

Read a second letter to the editor.

15 High Street
Westvale Village, IL 55555
April 19, 2001

Letters to the Editor
The Sentinel
500 Main Drive
Westvale Village, IL 55555

Dear Editor:

I support Mark Lewis's opinions about skateboarders. I agree that it is unfair to label skateboarders as troublemakers. I also agree that the bill that allows skateboarders to use the park is a good idea.

The park is safer than the street or mall parking lots, where some skateboarders continue to go. However, the park paths were not built for skateboarding. Huge oak trees line these paths. Roots from these trees have pushed up the ground in many spots. As a result, the paths are not as smooth as they could be. The trees are also a danger to skateboarders who wipe out near them. Finally, as Mark pointed out in his letter, some people are not happy that skateboarders are using the park at all. For these reasons, I think that the town should construct a skateboard park.

A national group that promotes skateboarding reports that 1,000 new skateboard parks have been built in cities and towns across the country in the last 18 months. Our community should follow the national **trend** to provide skateboarders with a safe, modern, well-designed park. At the town meeting, several parents of skateboarders asked the town to raise funds to build a skateboard park. The area around the Old Mill, along the river, would be a perfect **site**.

I am a member of a committee, led by Michael Alfonso, the director of the town Recreation Department. Last month we toured skateboard parks in neighboring towns to decide what we would like to have in our skateboard park. Then Mr. Alfonso contacted a park designer. The cost of a 10,000 square foot skateboard park with rails, steps, benches, ledges, and ramps will be about $185,000.

Some townspeople oppose the skateboard park because they think that skateboarding is too dangerous. Yet the town spends thousands of dollars each year for other sports, such as football, basketball, and baseball. According to the National Safety Council, more children are injured playing these sports than are injured skateboarding. Skateboarders are just like other athletes who want to practice their sport in a safe environment. Everyone should support the construction of the skateboard park.

Yours truly,

Angie Diaz

Angie Diaz

Using a fact-and-opinion chart

Fill in the fact-and-opinion chart with facts and opinions from the second letter to the editor.

FACT Can it be proved, checked, or tested? Is it something someone knows from experience?	OPINION Is it what someone believes, thinks, or feels?

Check Your Understanding

Think about what you've read. Then answer these questions.

1. From the information in Mark Lewis's letter, you can tell that Mark probably
   Ⓐ is the best skateboarder in Westvale Village.
   Ⓑ wears a helmet when he skateboards.
   Ⓒ plays baseball, soccer, and football.
   Ⓓ is rude to joggers.

2. How would you expect a hoodlum to act?
   Ⓐ like a criminal   Ⓒ like a movie star
   Ⓑ like an athlete   Ⓓ like a friend

3. In Mark's letter, the words *cast a dark shadow upon* suggest that
   Ⓐ skateboarders block the sun for others.
   Ⓑ skateboarders prefer to skate when it's dark.
   Ⓒ skateboarders have a bad reputation.
   Ⓓ skateboarders are cruel.

4. In Mark's letter, which of these words is a synonym for the word *inconsiderate*?
   Ⓐ recent   Ⓒ unfair
   Ⓑ dark   Ⓓ thoughtless

5. People who want to ban skateboarders from the park probably think that
   Ⓐ skateboarding is a great sport.
   Ⓑ all skateboarders should be arrested.
   Ⓒ only soccer should be allowed in the park.
   Ⓓ skateboarders should find another place to practice.

6. When people follow a trend, they
   Ⓐ march in a parade to support a cause.
   Ⓑ do what others are doing.
   Ⓒ walk along a park path.
   Ⓓ use a string or rope to find their way.

7. According to Angie Diaz, why are the park paths not as smooth as they could be?
   Ⓐ Skateboarders have damaged the paths.
   Ⓑ Joggers have worn them down.
   Ⓒ Tree roots have pushed up the ground.
   Ⓓ The Park Commission has refused to construct new paths.

8. Which of these details from Mark's letter is a fact?
   Ⓐ Last year, the Park Commission passed a bill.
   Ⓑ All the skateboarders I know appreciate having a place to skateboard.
   Ⓒ Most people believe that it makes sense for skateboarders to use the park.
   Ⓓ This action is unfair.

9. Which of these details from Angie's letter is an opinion?
   Ⓐ Huge oak trees line these paths.
   Ⓑ . . . several parents of skateboarders asked the town to raise funds to build a skateboard park.
   Ⓒ . . . Michael Alfonso, the director of the town Recreation Department.
   Ⓓ The park is safer than the street or mall parking lots, . . .

10. According to Angie, in what way are skateboarders different from athletes who play football, basketball, and baseball?
    Ⓐ Skateboarders suffer less injuries.
    Ⓑ Skateboarders wear safety gear.
    Ⓒ Skateboarders cause more trouble.
    Ⓓ Skateboarders want to practice in a safe environment.

11. Angie Diaz's letter is mostly about
- (A) providing a safe place for skateboarders to practice.
- (B) the dangers of skateboarding in the park.
- (C) the trouble skateboarders cause in the community.
- (D) the cost of skateboarding equipment.

12. Angie Diaz's main purpose for writing is to
- (A) describe the dangers of skateboarding in the park.
- (B) explain how to solve problems between skateboarders and other members of the community.
- (C) persuade readers to support the construction of a skateboard park.
- (D) tell an entertaining story about skateboarders.

Extend Your Learning

- *Write a Letter to the Editor*

  In a group, brainstorm topics about an issue that concerns you and other young people in your community. Choose the issue that you feel most strongly about and that you know the most facts about. List your opinions and any facts you know in a fact-and-opinion chart. You may wish to do more research to learn additional facts about the issue. Then use the details in your fact-and-opinion chart to write a letter to the editor of your school paper or your community paper. Be sure to use business letter form, as shown in the letters to the editor in this lesson.

- *Read and Compare Letters to the Editor*

  With a partner, find two or three letters to the editor, on the same topic, in a magazine, your school newspaper, or the community newspaper. Fill out a separate fact-and-opinion chart for each letter. Then use the completed charts to compare and contrast the facts and opinions each writer used. Decide which letter was most effective and why.

- *Research Attitudes Towards Sports in the Community*

  Conduct a survey to learn how adults and young people in your community feel about different sports, including traditional sports, such as baseball, football, soccer, and ice hockey; and newer, less traditional sports, such as skateboarding, inline skating, and snowboarding. Ask at least five adults and five young people their opinions and attitudes toward these sports. Record their responses in a chart. Then compare your results with the results of your classmates.

LESSON 10 Identifying Author's Purpose

Learn About Identifying Author's Purpose

*Thinking about
the strategy*

Authors always write for a reason, even if the reason is to jot down ideas an author doesn't want to forget. The reason an author writes is called **author's purpose**. Authors usually write for one of four reasons.

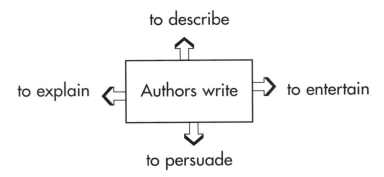

An author who writes to describe uses vivid details to help readers picture a person, place, or thing. An author who writes to entertain uses words and ideas that readers will enjoy. An author who wants to persuade, or convince, you to believe something or do something may offer strong evidence that supports the author's opinions. An author who writes to explain includes facts and details that help you to understand a subject.

Authors often have more than one reason for writing. To identify the author's main purpose, pay attention to key ideas and details. Then ask yourself, "What is the author trying to do?"

Studying a model

Read the paragraph and the notes beside it.

The author introduces the topic, volcanoes, with an opinion.

The author provides information about how a volcanic eruption begins.

The author gives more facts and details about volcanoes.

A volcanic eruption is one of the most spectacular events in nature. While scientists may not completely understand the forces that cause a volcano to erupt, they do have a good idea of what occurs during an eruption. Deep inside the earth, hot melted rock, called magma, produces a large amount of gas. The gas and the magma mix, and then begin to rise toward the earth's surface. As the gas and magma rise, the heat causes surrounding solid rock to melt. This forms a reservoir, or holding space, called the magma chamber.

Learn About a Graphic Organizer

Understanding an author's purpose questionnaire

You can use an **author's purpose questionnaire** to explore key ideas and identify details that suggest an author's purpose. An author's purpose questionnaire is useful when trying to identify author's purpose in fiction and nonfiction selections.

Here is an author's purpose questionnaire for the paragraph on page 94. As you can see, the questions help the reader focus on key ideas and details in the paragraph. The answers lead the reader to understand what the author is trying to do and to determine the author's purpose.

QUESTION	ANSWER	
What does the author say?	Volcanic eruptions are spectacular.	*Write answers to the questions on the left.*
What do others say and do?	Scientists do not completely understand what makes a volcano erupt, but they do have a good idea of what occurs during an eruption.	
What are key ideas and details?	Magma, hot melted rock inside the earth, produces gas. The magma mixes with gas. The rising magma and gas melt rocks, forming the magma chamber.	
What is the author trying to do?	The author wants the reader to understand how a volcano erupts.	*Use your answers to help you decide the author's purpose.*
Author's Purpose	to explain	

When you complete an author's purpose questionnaire, you identify the author's main purpose, or reason, for writing. This can help you decide how you will read and what your purpose for reading will be.

The author's purpose is to explain something.
How should I read this? What is my purpose for reading?
I will read slowly to understand. I want to learn how volcanoes erupt.

As you read, ask yourself

- What is the author trying to do?
- What key ideas and details suggest the author's purpose?

Learn About a Form of Writing

A **personal narrative** is a story about something that is meaningful to the author and that has made a difference in the author's life.

A personal narrative usually has these features.

- It is told in the first person, using the personal pronoun *I*.
- It uses a narrative, or story, form.
- It is usually told to entertain, but may be told to describe or explain.

Read this paragraph from a personal narrative written by George Pete.

> When it came time to sign me up for little league, Dad said that I didn't have to play if I didn't want to. However, the look on his face was so hopeful that I said, "Sure, sign me up." I spent most of the season on the bench. I was a terrible batter, and a worse fielder. Somehow, in spite of me, my team made it to the playoffs. In the last game, the coach put me in center field. I just hoped no one would hit a ball in my direction. With one out to go to end the game and win the playoffs, I heard the crack of the bat. The ball soared toward me. I jumped, put up my mitt, and caught the ball! Suddenly everyone was hugging me. Then I was put up on the coach's shoulder and paraded around the field. I'm still not crazy about sports, but being a hero is cool.

You can use an author's purpose questionnaire for a personal narrative. Here is a filled-in author's purpose questionnaire for the paragraph above.

QUESTION	ANSWER
What does the author say?	He spent most of the season on the bench.
What do others say and do?	Coach put him in a playoff game. Child on other team hit the ball to center field.
What are key ideas and details?	He catches the ball and gets treated like a hero.
What is the author trying to do?	The author wants to tell a story about a meaningful event in his life.
Author's Purpose	to entertain

Prepare for the Reading Selection

Gaining knowledge

For most children, learning to ride a bike is part of growing up, like learning to walk. Children and bicycles seem to go together. In the late 1800s, however, when bicycles became popular, they were made for adults. Then, in the early 1900s, adults turned their attention to an exciting new means of transportation: the automobile. As adults lost interest in bicycles, bicycle manufacturers focused their attention on children. Of course, children are typically rough on their things, so children's bicycles were built tougher and sturdier than earlier models. Arnold, Schwinn & Company, which was founded in 1895, was one bicycle company that began making affordable bikes for American children. By the 1950s, a Schwinn bike was on just about every child's wish list. On the following pages, you will read a personal narrative about wanting a bicycle.

Learn Vocabulary

Understanding vocabulary

The boxed words below are **boldfaced** in the selection. Learn the meaning of each word. Then write the word that completes the sentence.

glum
dramatic
reckless
tinged
issue
submit
applaud
entrants

1. I know that you tried hard, and I _____ your efforts.

2. Crossing the street without checking for cars is foolish and

   _____ .

3. The first one hundred _____ in the race will receive free T-shirts.

4. The most _____ moment in the book is when the hero rescues a child from the runaway horse.

5. The students will discuss the _____ of whether skateboarding should be allowed on school property.

6. Their joy was _____ with the fear of what might happen next.

7. Peter was so _____ that none of us could cheer him up.

8. We have until Friday to _____ our project ideas to Mr. Soong.

Read the first part of the personal narrative "The Lesson."

The Lesson

I stood in the middle of the kitchen, waiting for a reply. Before my mother answered, she looked at my dad. Then she turned to me and said, "No. I'm sorry, but the answer is no, you cannot have a two-wheeler."

It was the answer I'd expected, but not the answer that I wanted.

"Why not?" I pleaded.

"For the same reason that we've said no every time you've asked," my dad said. "It's not safe to ride a bike in the city."

"But Virginia has a bike," I said. "And so does Michele and Jimmy and Frankie. Everyone has a bike but me. It's not fair." I wanted to shout and stomp my feet, but I didn't. I had more brains than that.

My mother put her head down in her hands. My father got up and went to the mirror to retie his bow tie. It was time for him to go back to work. He was a waiter at a restaurant in the city. Between 2:00 P.M. and 5:00 P.M., the restaurant was closed so my father walked home to rest and spend time with my mother and us. Then he went back for the dinner rush. By the time he came home again, my sisters and I were asleep.

Before my dad left, he looked into my room. I was on the bed, feeling **glum**.

"It's not the end of the world, Susan," he said. "You'll survive without a bike."

"I know, Daddy," I said. "But how will I ever learn to ride. I'm the only person in the whole fifth grade that can't ride a two-wheeler. It's un-American!"

My father chuckled, not in a mean way, but in a way that let me know I was being **dramatic**. Perhaps I was, but I didn't understand my parents' reasoning. They knew how responsible I was. They knew that I always followed rules. I would never be **reckless**. It wasn't in my nature. Still they wouldn't budge.

That night, I had trouble sleeping. For awhile, I just lay there, comforted by the sound of the radio and my mother's voice as she sang along to the top ten songs of 1956. Before long, I heard the click of my father's heels as he walked up the front stairs of our building, and then the sound of his key in the lock. I heard him go into his room, which was right next to ours, to change. My mom followed after him. "Is there any way we can get her a bike?" my mother asked.

When my dad answered, his voice was **tinged** with sadness. "There's no money for a bike, Olga," he said. "You know that."

"Maybe we should tell her the real reason she can't have a bike," Mom said. "She'll understand. It would make more sense to her."

"No," my father said. The conversation was over.

On the way to school the next morning, I thought about what I had learned the night before. I still wanted a bike, but now I knew better than to ask for one.

I was never one to hang on to bad feelings, so by the time I got to school, I had tucked the whole **issue** of the bike in a corner of my mind where it wouldn't bother me. It didn't stay there for long.

"Class," Mrs. James, my fifth-grade teacher, said. "Miss Miller has come to tell us about a contest that the library is sponsoring."

Completing an author's purpose questionnaire

Some of the author's purpose questionnaire has been filled in. Add more information from the first part of the personal narrative.

QUESTION	ANSWER
What does the author say?	She expects her parents to say no about a bike. She hopes they will say yes. She wants to shout and stomp her feet, but doesn't.
What do others say and do?	Her mother says, "No . . . you cannot have a two-wheeler."
What are key ideas and details?	
What is the author trying to do?	

Read the second part of the personal narrative "The Lesson."

Miss Miller was the children's librarian at the public library. She quickly explained the contest rules. "Every child in grades 5 through 8 can **submit** an essay about what the library means to him or her. Winners will be announced on Awards Day. The grand prize is a brand new Schwinn bicycle."

Virginia turned around in her seat and gave me a big smile.

My friend Jimmy, who sat behind me, leaned forward and whispered, "Looks like you'll be getting a bike this year after all."

I knew what they were thinking. I had won every writing prize the school had given out in the last three years. I had also won two essay contests sponsored by the library and the local newspaper.

"Why are you so happy?" my mother asked when I came through the door that afternoon wearing a huge grin. I was about to tell her when I realized something. All along my parents had said I couldn't have a bike because it was too dangerous. What excuse would they give for changing their minds when I won the bike? I decided to keep the contest a secret.

On Awards Day, we gathered in the school hall—parents, teachers, and students. For the first hour, teachers from each class gave out the usual end-of-the-year awards. Jimmy got the fifth-grade perfect attendance award. Virginia got the award for being the most helpful student. I got two awards, one for math and one for English. Normally, I would have been thrilled, but all I could think of was how it would feel to win a bike.

Then Miss Miller walked onto the stage. "I want to **applaud** all the **entrants**," she said. "However, we could only have one grand prize winner, and that person is . . . Michele Cefalo."

I was stunned. Michele already had a bike.

I don't remember much more about that afternoon. I know I congratulated Michele and tried to act happy for her.

Later that night, I again overheard my parents talking.

"She must have had her heart set on that bike," my dad said.

"I hope she never finds out why she didn't win," my mom said.

"What exactly did her teacher say to you?" my dad asked.

Mom was talking low, but the anger in her voice was clear. "Mrs. James said that Susan wrote the best essay. However, the teachers who judged the contest felt that it was time for Susan to learn a lesson about life. They decided she should know how it feels to lose. Do you believe that?"

I guess I was too young to understand the lesson. All I felt was confused and hurt. I cried a little, and then I fell asleep. When I woke up, the memory of what had happened was like a bruise. Like all the bruises I ever received, it soon faded.

I never asked for a bicycle again. When I was sixteen, I borrowed a friend's bike and taught myself to ride, but I've never been comfortable on a bike, and I've never had a bike of my own.

Using an author's purpose questionnaire

Fill in the author's purpose questionnaire for the second part of the personal narrative. Use the questionnaire that you filled in for Part One to help you identify the author's purpose for the whole selection.

QUESTION	ANSWER
What does the author say?	
What do others say and do?	
What are key ideas and details?	
What is the author trying to do?	
Author's Purpose	

Check Your Understanding

Think about what you've read. Then answer these questions.

1. The author wrote this personal narrative mainly to
   - Ⓐ explain why some children never learn to ride a bike.
   - Ⓑ describe a Schwinn bicycle.
   - Ⓒ entertain readers with a meaningful story from her life.
   - Ⓓ convince readers that adults are not always fair.

2. Which of these does the author use to help her achieve her purpose for writing?
   - Ⓐ lively dialogue, interesting characters, and a clear sequence of events
   - Ⓑ detailed descriptions of different bike models
   - Ⓒ opinions about how children should be treated
   - Ⓓ facts and details about when and how children learn to ride a bike

3. Susan's dad could probably tell she was feeling glum because she looked
   - Ⓐ excited.   Ⓒ bored.
   - Ⓑ unhappy.   Ⓓ afraid.

4. According to Susan, what made her different from most other fifth-grade children?
   - Ⓐ She lived in a dangerous city.
   - Ⓑ Her father was not home to have dinner with the family.
   - Ⓒ She had never owned a bike.
   - Ⓓ She didn't know how to ride a two-wheeler.

5. Susan's parents do not get her a bike because
   - Ⓐ Susan does not know how to ride a bike.
   - Ⓑ they can't afford to buy her a bike.
   - Ⓒ none of the other parents let their children ride bikes in the city.
   - Ⓓ they expect Susan to win a bike.

6. From the details in the personal narrative, you can figure out that Susan does not
   - Ⓐ respect her parents.
   - Ⓑ do well in school.
   - Ⓒ like to dwell on bad feelings.
   - Ⓓ follow rules that don't make sense.

7. A synonym for the word *issue* is
   - Ⓐ argument.   Ⓒ conversation.
   - Ⓑ emotion.   Ⓓ subject.

8. Which of these statements best summarizes Part One of "The Lesson"?
   - Ⓐ Susan overhears her parents talking and finally understands why they won't let her have a bike.
   - Ⓑ Susan gets angry with her parents when they tell her she can't have a bike.
   - Ⓒ Susan figures out a way to get a bike.
   - Ⓓ Susan begs her parents to buy her a bike.

9. Susan planned to submit her essay. She planned to
   - Ⓐ write her essay.
   - Ⓑ read her essay.
   - Ⓒ turn in her essay.
   - Ⓓ revise her essay.

10. Which of these sentences from the personal narrative is an opinion?
    - Ⓐ Miss Miller was the children's librarian at the public library.
    - Ⓑ The grand prize is a brand new Schwinn bicycle.
    - Ⓒ Jimmy got the fifth-grade perfect attendance award.
    - Ⓓ She must have had her heart set on that bike.

11. Which of these events happens first in the personal narrative?

   Ⓐ   Susan learns to ride a bike.

   Ⓑ   Miss Miller announces the winner of the essay contest.

   Ⓒ   Susan tries to be happy for Michele.

   Ⓓ   Susan overhears her parents talking about Miss James.

12. Which of these is a comparison called a simile?

   Ⓐ   . . . the anger in her voice was clear.

   Ⓑ   All I felt was confused and hurt.

   Ⓒ   . . . the memory of what had happened was like a bruise.

   Ⓓ   Like all the bruises I ever received, it soon faded.

Extend Your Learning

• *Write a Personal Narrative*

List events in your life when you learned an important lesson. Choose the event that has the most meaning for you. Then write a personal narrative about this event. Remember that a personal narrative has all the elements of a good story, including a setting, characters, and a series of events that lead to a conclusion. Include vivid and precise details that will help readers understand why this event was important to you. Try to write lively dialogue that will add interest and that will make your narrative enjoyable to read.

• *Research the History of Bicycles*

With a partner, do research to learn more about the history and development of the bicycle. Look in encyclopedias and on the Internet for information. Try to find at least three different references on the topic. As you read, fill in an author's purpose questionnaire for each reference. Then use the questionnaire to identify the author's purpose of the article or book.

• *Explain an Event in Nature*

In a group, brainstorm different natural disasters or weather events, such as volcanoes and hurricanes. Choose an event to research and write one or two paragraphs to explain or to describe this event. Keep your purpose for writing in mind as you decide what kinds of details to include. You may wish to reread the passage on page 94 for an example of a paragraph that explains. Share your passage with your group.

Interpreting Figurative Language

Learn About Interpreting Figurative Language

*Thinking about
the strategy*

Authors understand that readers will better enjoy and understand what they are reading if readers can picture what an author is describing. To help readers create mental pictures, authors use **figurative language**. Figurative language has meaning beyond the dictionary meaning of the words. Types of figurative language include similes, metaphors, and personification.

Figurative Language		Example	What it means
Simile	Compares two unlike things, using the word *like* or *as*.	Her smile was like sunshine after a week of rain.	Her smile was warm, bright, and welcomed.
Metaphor	Compares two things without *like* or *as*. Says one thing is another.	The man's weathered face was a map of lines and wrinkles.	The man's face was marked with lines and wrinkles, in the way a map is marked with roads, rivers, and other features.
Personification	Gives human traits to animals, objects, things in nature, and ideas.	The warm sun reached out and hugged the child.	The warmth of the sun comforted the child, the way a parent's arms comfort a child.

Authors use similes, metaphors, and personification to make their writing more interesting and their ideas easier to understand. To interpret different types of figurative language, try to picture what is being compared. Then ask, "What do the ideas and pictures communicate? How do they make me feel?"

Studying a model

Read the paragraph and the notes beside it.

The author uses a simile that compares the people to worker ants.

The author uses personification to compare the sun to a person, and a metaphor to compare a gray sky and cold wind to companions.

People moved along the sidewalk like worker ants with one single purpose. No one stopped to smile or say, "Good day." No one seemed to care or even notice that among them were men and women in need of a helping hand. The sun, recognizing it could not penetrate such hardhearted souls, retreated. The dingy gray sky and bitter cold wind were more suitable companions.

Learn About a Graphic Organizer

Understanding a figurative language chart

A **figurative language chart** will help you identify figurative language and interpret its meaning. You can use a figurative language chart when reading short stories, myths, fables, poetry, and other selections.

Here is a figurative language chart for the paragraph on page 104. The chart identifies the types of figurative language used in the paragraph, and what is being compared. It also explains what the figurative language means.

List the figurative language and identify the type. *Tell the things being compared.* *Explain the figurative language.*

Figurative Language		What Is Being Compared	What It Means
People moved . . . like worker ants	Simile	people and worker ants	The people moved along as if by instinct. Nothing distracts them from their purpose.
The sun, recognizing it could not penetrate . . . , retreated.	Personification	The sun is compared to a wise person.	The sun disappears.
The dingy gray sky . . . suitable companions.	Metaphor	gray sky, bitter cold wind, and companions	The gray sky and cold wind match the cold mood of the people.

When you complete a figurative language chart, you have a better understanding of what an author is saying.

What does the author want me to understand about the people?
The people are interested only in themselves and are insensitive to the needs of others.

As you read, ask yourself

- Is the figurative language a simile, a metaphor, or personification?
- What mental picture does the figurative language create?
- What message does this mental picture send? How does this mental picture make me feel?

Learn About a Form of Writing

Focusing on a poem

A **poem** is a word picture that a poet creates to express an idea or emotion. Poets choose words because of how they sound and because of the images they call to mind. Sounds and images are important to the meaning of a poem. Because sounds and images can affect people in different ways, a poem can mean different things to different people.

A poem often has these features.

- It contains figurative language and vivid images.
- It is arranged in lines and stanzas.
- It tells a story, expresses an idea, or presents one clear image.
- Its purpose is to entertain or express an idea.

Here is a poem. Think about the picture it creates in your mind.

The Garden

The garden is a gentle sea at rest
Beside the coast of a minor country.
Its flowers are like colorful waves
Swept by soft winds
Beneath a playful sun, hiding
Behind clouds going nowhere.

Organizing ideas in a figurative language chart

You can use a figurative language chart to identify and interpret figurative language in a poem. Here is a filled-in figurative language chart for the poem above.

Figurative Language		What Is Being Compared	What It Means
The garden is a gentle sea at rest	metaphor	garden and a peaceful sea	The garden reminds the poet of a quiet sea.
Its flowers are like colorful waves swept by soft winds	simile	flowers and waves	The flowers appear to move like ocean waves move.
a playful sun, hiding behind clouds	personification	The sun is compared to a playful child.	The sun goes behind a cloud.

Prepare for the Reading Selection

The poems you will read on the following pages are all about the same general topic. However, each poet approaches the topic in a different way, using different poetic devices, or tools. These devices include rhyme, rhythm, and imagery.

Rhyme is the repetition of the same sound, usually at the end of lines. Sometimes, poets use internal rhyme. Then words within a line rhyme.

Rhythm is the repetition of a beat. Rhyme and rhythm can give poetry a musical quality. Poems that are written in free verse do not have a regular rhyme or rhythm pattern.

Imagery is language that appeals to the five senses of sight, hearing, sound, taste, and touch. Imagery allows the poet to create a word picture that readers can see, enjoy, and understand. Imagery often contains similes, metaphors, and personification.

Learn Vocabulary

Understanding vocabulary

The boxed words below are **boldfaced** in the selections. Learn the meaning of each word. Then write the word that matches the clue.

nook
drowsy
surge
splendors
scimitar
vague
mystic
eternal
dome

1. This is a high rounded top of a building. _____

2. This means forever. _____

3. This is another word for a cozy corner. _____

4. This is a rush of water. _____

5. This is another word for unclear. _____

6. This means tired and sleepy. _____

7. Great works of art might be described this way.

   _____

8. This is mysterious. _____

9. This is a curved sword worn by Asian soldiers.

   _____

Read the poems "The Sun Has Set," "Full Moon," "Nightfall," and "Phases of the Moon."

The Sun Has Set

The sun has set, and the long grass now
Waves dreamily in the evening wind:
And the wild bird has flown from that old gray stone
In some warm **nook** a couch to find.

In all the lonely landscape round
I hear not light and hear no sound.
Except the wind that far away
Come sighing o'er the healthy sea.

Emily Brontë

Full Moon

One night as Dick lay half asleep,
  Into his **drowsy** eyes
A great still light began to creep
  From out the silent skies.
It was the lovely moon's, for when
  He raised his dreamy head,
Her **surge** of silver filled his pane
  And streamed across his bed.
So, for a while, each gazed at each—
  Dick and the solemn moon—
Till, climbing slowly on her way,
  She vanished, and was gone.

Walter de la Mare

Nightfall

As evening **splendors** fade
  From yonder sky afar,
The Night pins on her dark
  Robe with a large bright star,
And the new moon hangs like
  A high-grown **scimitar**.

Vague in the **mystic** room
  This side the paling west,
The Tulledegas* loom
  In an **eternal** rest,
And one by one the lamps are lit
In the **dome** of the Infinite**.

Alexander Lawrence Posey

*The Tulledega Hills are in Oklahoma. As night falls and the sun sets in the west, the outline of the hills becomes vague, or difficult for the poet to see.

**Infinite here means the sky or the universe.

Phases of the Moon

Once upon a time I heard
That the flying moon was a Phoenix* bird;
Thus she sails through windy skies,
Thus in the willow's arms she lies;
Turn to the East or turn to the West
In many trees she makes her nest.
When she's but a pearly thread
Look among birch leaves overhead;
When she hides in yellow smoke
Look in a thunder-smitten** oak;
But in May when the moon is full,
Bright as water and white as wool,
Look for her where she loves to be,
Asleep in a high magnolia tree.

Elinor Wylie

Completing a figurative language chart

Fill in the figurative language chart for the poems in Part One. Some examples have been filled in. Write what is being compared and what you think the words mean.

Figurative Language		What Is Being Compared	What It Means
long grass waves dreamily	personification	The long grass is given the traits of a sleepy person.	long grass moves in a slow dreamy motion like people move when sleepy
wind comes sighing	personification	The wind is given the ability to breathe.	wind makes a soft sighing sound like a person makes
The Night pins on her dark/Robe with a large bright star,	personification		
And the new moon hangs like/ A high-grown scimitar.	simile		
the flying moon was a Phoenix bird;	metaphor		

Read the poem "Wynken, Blynken, and Nod."

Wynken, Blynken, and Nod

Wynken, Blynken, and Nod one night
Sailed off in a wooden shoe,—
Sailed on a river of crystal light
Into a sea of dew.
"Where are you going, and what do you wish?"
The old moon asked the three.
"We have come to fish for the herring fish
That live in this beautiful sea;
Nets of silver and gold have we!"
    Said Wynken,
    Blynken,
    and Nod.

The old moon laughed and sang a song,
As they rocked in the wooden shoe;
And the wind that sped them all night long
Ruffled the waves of dew.
The little stars were the herring fish
That lived in the beautiful sea—
"Now cast your nets wherever you wish,—
Never afeared are we!"
So cried the stars to the fishermen three,
    Wynken,
    Blynken,
    And Nod.

All night long their nets they threw
To the stars in the twinkling foam,—
Then down from the skies came the wooden shoe,
Bringing the fishermen home:
'Twas all so pretty a sail, it seemed
As if it could not be;
And some folk thought 'twas a dream they'd dreamed
Of sailing that beautiful sea;
But I shall name you the fishermen three:
    Wynken,
    Blynken,
    And Nod.

Wynken and Blynken are two little eyes,
And Nod is a little head,
And the wooden shoe that sailed the skies
Is a wee one's trundle-bed;
So shut your eyes while Mother sings
Of wonderful sights that be,
And you shall see the beautiful things
As you rock in the misty sea
Where the old shoe rocked the fishermen three:—
    Wynken,
    Blynken,
    And Nod.

Eugene Field

Using a figurative language chart

Use details from the poem "Wynken, Blynken, and Nod" to fill in the figurative language chart.

Figurative Language		What Is Being Compared	What It Means

Check Your Understanding

Think about what you've read. Then answer these questions.

1. In what way is "The Sun Has Set" different from the other poems in Part One.
    - (A) It rhymes.
    - (B) It is about night.
    - (C) It has two stanzas.
    - (D) It describes the sun and moon.

2. In "The Sun Has Set," the wild bird searches for a nook. The bird is probably looking for
    - (A) a soft couch.
    - (B) a cozy tree hole.
    - (C) a grassy hill.
    - (D) the sea.

3. In "Nightfall," the moon is compared to
    - (A) a sword.
    - (B) a dome.
    - (C) a lamp.
    - (D) a star.

4. In "Nightfall," you can tell that the word *loom* means
    - (A) "a weaving machine."
    - (B) "to rise from nowhere."
    - (C) "to threaten."
    - (D) "to be on the horizon."

5. The speaker of "Nightfall" refers to the Tulledega Hills as eternal. Something eternal
    - (A) lasts forever.
    - (B) is covered with grass.
    - (C) is low and rolling.
    - (D) never speaks.

6. In "Full Moon," Dick's eyes are drowsy. Another word for *drowsy* is
    - (A) closed.
    - (B) open.
    - (C) sleepy.
    - (D) sparkling.

7. Which statement best expresses the main idea of the story told in "Full Moon"?
    - (A) Dick was almost asleep when the bright light of the full moon rising woke him.
    - (B) Dick fell asleep as the light of the full moon came through his window.
    - (C) Dick gazed at the full moon, but the moon did not gaze back.
    - (D) Dick lifted up his head just as the light of the full moon came through his window.

8. In "Phases of the Moon," the moon is compared to all of the following except
    - (A) thread.
    - (B) wool.
    - (C) smoke.
    - (D) a bird.

9. According to the author of "Phases of the Moon," where is the last place you will find the moon?
    - (A) in the willow's arms
    - (B) in a high magnolia tree
    - (C) in a thunder-smitten oak
    - (D) among birch leaves

10. In "Wynken, Blynken, and Nod," what conclusion can you draw about real herring fish?
    - (A) Their scales sparkle like stars.
    - (B) They are fast swimmers.
    - (C) They make a laughing sound.
    - (D) They cannot be caught.

11. In "Wynken, Blynken, and Nod," Wynken, Blynken, and Nod are actually

Ⓐ a child's eyes and head.

Ⓑ a mother and her two children.

Ⓒ three herring fish.

Ⓓ the moon and two little stars.

12. What is the author's purpose in "Wynken, Blynken, and Nod"?

Ⓐ to tell a true story about three fishers

Ⓑ to explain how the stars got in the sky

Ⓒ to entertain readers with a fantasy story

Ⓓ to describe the night sky

Extend Your Learning

• *Read and Recite a Poem*

Make a list of topics suggested by the poems you read, such as sunset, the moon, stars, nightfall, and sleep. Then find another poem related to one of the topics. As you read the poem, use a figurative language chart to identify and interpret the figurative language in the poem. Practice reciting the poem. When you are ready, recite the poem for the class.

• *Research the Phases of the Moon*

Work with a partner to learn more about the phases of the moon. Use library resources and the Internet to find information. Share what you learn in a poster or brief report. Try to incorporate verses from Elinor Wylie's poem "Phases of the Moon" in your poster or report.

• *Write a Poem*

In a group, write a poem about sunset, nightfall, or the moon. Before you write, brainstorm a list of things you might compare to the setting sun, the night sky, or the moon. As you compose your poem, use your list of comparisons to create similes, metaphors, and personification. Then get together with other groups to present your poems at a class poetry reading.

Summarizing

Learn About Summarizing

Thinking about the strategy

A summary is a brief retelling of a piece of fiction or nonfiction. When you **summarize**, you use your own words and the author's words to retell the most important points of a story, an article, or a book.

To summarize a story, pay attention to the setting, the main characters, the story problem, and the solution. Then retell only the main points of the story. Do not include unimportant or minor details.

Studying a model

Read the story and the notes beside it.

Tia is the main character.

The details about the autocycle, the space park, a personal robot, and the planet Earth suggest that the setting of this story is sometime in the future on a planet that is not Earth.

The story problem revolves around Tia's plans to go out and her mother's orders to clean her room without the help of RM, her personal robot.

Tia's solution is to make cleaning her room the old-fashioned way as much fun as possible.

Tia was about to leave her house when her mom stopped her. "Did you clean your room and do your homework?" she asked.

"I finished most of my homework," Tia said sweetly. "I was just going to ride my new autocycle at the space park."

"Sorry," Tia's mom said. "You know the rules."

Tia frowned and stomped down to her room. "And I expect you to clean, not RM," her mother called after her.

"She's so old-fashioned," Tia mumbled. Now, instead of commanding her personal robot RM to clean her room, Tia would have to do the vacuuming and picking up by herself. "What good is a personal robot if you can't have it do chores? I might as well live on Earth back in the twentieth century," Tia grumbled.

Then Tia got an idea. She programmed RM to search his database for the clothing styles and music of 1999 Earth children. Tia reviewed the search results. Then she pressed several command buttons on RM's console. Seconds later, Tia was dressed in a pair of dark blue jeans and a T-shirt as she dusted and vacuumed to the beat of a singing group called N'Sync.

"Well," Tia said cheerfully to RM, whose screen was blinking in time to the music, "maybe when I'm done, you can call up a twentieth-century snack. Having to push these vacuum buttons is making me hungry!"

Learn About a Graphic Organizer

Understanding a story map

A **story map** can help you identify the main story elements and how they relate to each other. You can use the notes in a completed story map to develop a summary of the story.

Here is a story map for the story on page 114.

Tell whom the story is mostly about.

CHARACTERS
Tia, a young girl
RM, Tia's personal robot

Tell where and when the story takes place.

SETTING
planet in outer space
sometime in the future

Tell the problem the main character faces.

PROBLEM
Tia is about to go to ride her autocycle at the space park when her mother tells her she has to stay home to clean her room without the help of her personal robot RM.

Tell the events that show how the main character deals with the problem.

MAIN EVENTS
Tia grumbles about having to do chores the old-fashioned way.
Tia programs RM to search for the clothing and music of 1999 Earth children.
Tia dresses in jeans and a T-shirt and listens to the music of N'Sync.

Tell how the story problem is solved and how the story ends.

SOLUTION
Tia still has to clean her room, but by dressing like a young girl from Earth in the year 1999 and listening to music, Tia finds a way to make the job fun.

What is a summary of the story?

Tia lives on a planet in outer space sometime in the future. Tia's plan to ride her autocycle at the space park changes when her mother tells her to clean her room without the help of RM, her personal robot. Tia grumbles about having to do chores the old-fashioned way, but then she finds a way to make the experience fun. She commands RM to dress her the way children on Earth dressed in 1999 and to play music from the same time period.

As you read, ask yourself

- What are the main story elements?
- How can I use the main story elements to summarize the story?

Learn About a Form of Writing

Focusing on a fable

A **fable** is a short story with a simple plot that teaches a lesson.

A fable often has these special characteristics.

- It contains animals that talk and act the way people do.
- It teaches a lesson about the way people should behave in real life.

Here is a familiar fable.

> A wolf secretly watched a flock of sheep grazing on a hillside. The shepherd was so watchful that the wolf did not have a chance to get near the sheep. One day, the wolf found an old sheepskin that he slipped on over his own furry coat. Disguised as a sheep, the wolf wandered among the flock. Not even the watchful shepherd recognized him. When the sheep were locked up for the night, the wolf was with them. Later, the shepherd got hungry and went down to where the sheep slept. The shepherd grabbed the wolf, thinking it was the fattest sheep, and plopped him in the pot for stew.

Organizing ideas in a story map

Here is a filled-in story map for the above fable that can help you summarize the fable.

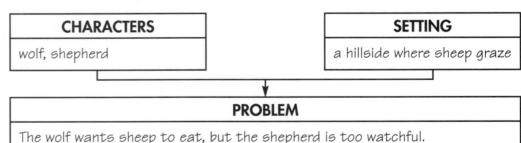

CHARACTERS	SETTING
wolf, shepherd	a hillside where sheep graze

PROBLEM

The wolf wants sheep to eat, but the shepherd is too watchful.

MAIN EVENTS

The wolf finds an old sheepskin that he uses to disguise himself as a sheep.
The wolf fools the shepherd and is able to wander freely among the flock.
The wolf is locked up with the sheep at night.

SOLUTION

The wolf's plan backfires when the hungry shepherd thinks the wolf is a sheep and plops him in the pot for stew.

Prepare for the Reading Selection

Gaining knowledge

The fable that you will read on the following pages takes place in ancient Rome. Thousands of years ago, the ancient Roman Empire covered a large portion of the world that is now occupied by parts of Europe, the Middle East, and Africa. At the head of the Roman Empire was an emperor, who was like a king. It was the custom to punish those who broke the law or who somehow offended the emperor. The prisoners were punished in a public arena. The arena was similar to our sports stadiums. However, instead of gathering to watch people play a sport, Romans often gathered to watch prisoners be put to death. The prisoner would be brought to the center of the arena. Soldiers would then release starving beasts, such as lions or tigers, into the arena. Without weapons, the prisoners could not defend themselves. Death was always the final outcome.

Learn Vocabulary

Understanding vocabulary

The boxed words below are **boldfaced** in the selection. Learn the meaning of each word. Then write the word beside its definition.

massive
responsibility
obstacles
relieved
fate
agony
affectionately
condemned

1. terrible pain and suffering _____

2. found guilty of a crime and sentenced _____

3. very large in size _____

4. what will happen to someone in the future _____

5. things that block the way _____

6. in a warm, friendly manner _____

7. duty _____

8. freed from worry _____

Read the first part of the fable "Androcles Meets the Lion."

Androcles Meets the Lion

One morning, a very long time ago, in a forest not far from the ancient city of Rome, a lion set out to find food for his family. Before he left, he spoke sternly to his three lively cubs and their mother. "Do not wander away from our den," he warned. "Roman soldiers have set traps all over the forest. They would like nothing more than to capture you for their arena games." Then, with a promise to return as soon as possible, the lion waved goodbye.

The night before, a windstorm had lifted several huge trees from their roots and toppled them to the ground. The **massive** trunks now stretched across the path, blocking the lion's way. The lion could easily have leaped over the trunks. However, since he was king of the forest, he felt that it was his **responsibility** to see that the path was free of **obstacles**. With a mighty roar, the lion lifted the tree trunks one by one and tossed them aside like matchsticks. Soon the path was clear, and the lion was once again on his way. He had not noticed that, as he worked, a sliver of wood had pierced his right front paw and was stuck there still.

Now it so happened that on the same morning, a slave named Androcles planned to escape his cruel master. First, he brought his master breakfast as usual. Then he helped his master bathe and dress. After that, he went out to work in the vegetable garden, just as he did every morning.

Two guards were posted at the garden gate to watch over Androcles. As the sun climbed higher in the sky, the guards became drowsy and fell asleep. Androcles was not surprised since the two lazy guards napped every day. While the guards slept, Androcles climbed over the garden wall and ran as fast as he could into the forest.

At first, Androcles was so **relieved** to be free that he did not think about the new dangers that he faced. Soon, the cawing and screeching and howling and hissing and buzzing and growling reminded him that the forest was home to many wild beasts. Even so, Androcles believed that he had a better chance at a happy life now. All he had to do was avoid being taken by Roman soldiers or attacked by a hungry lion or tiger.

Androcles kept running until he was deep in the forest. Although he knew he was taking a chance, he decided to stop and rest. He chose a spot that was camouflaged by a large mound of dead leaves, twigs, and vines. Certain that he was hidden from view, Androcles closed his eyes. In moments, the exhausted man was asleep.

As Androcles slept, two large hawks perched on a branch above him.

"He is in danger," one hawk said looking down on the sleeping Androcles.

"Soldiers are looking for him," the other hawk said.

"Can we help him?" the first hawk asked.

"His **fate** is in his own hands," the second hawk replied. Just then, there was a loud rustling in the bushes, and the hawks flew away.

Completing a story map

Review the first part of the fable to add details to this story map. Leave room in the main events frame to add details after reading the second part. Leave the solution frame blank for now.

CHARACTERS		SETTING
		a forest near ancient Rome

PROBLEM

Androcles wants to be free, so he escapes into the forest.

MAIN EVENTS

SOLUTION

Read the second part of the fable "Androcles Meets the Lion."

The sound of rustling leaves and the flapping of hawks' wings awakened Androcles. He was struggling to untangle himself from a leafy vine when he heard a disturbing sound.

"Ooh! Ow! What pain! What pain! Ooh! Ow! How it hurts! How it hurts!"

Someone was in trouble. Androcles peered around the mound of leaves where he had been sleeping to see who was moaning and groaning. When he did, he looked straight into the eyes of an enormous lion!

Androcles was about to faint from terror. "My life is over," he thought as he closed his eyes and waited for the lion to attack. Nothing happened. Androcles opened his eyes slowly. The lion was holding out his right front paw.

"Can you please help me?" the lion whimpered. The lion's paw was red and raw and throbbing in pain.

Androcles could not stand to watch even the smallest creature suffer. Forgetting his own fear, Androcles gently grasped the lion's paw. "You have a splinter," he told the lion. "I will have to pull it out. That will hurt, but then your paw will start to heal."

The lion nodded. "Do it," he told Androcles. "Nothing could hurt worse than this does." Androcles pulled out the thorn, which made the lion howl in **agony**.

"My life is surely over now," Androcles thought as he waited for the lion to attack. Instead, the grateful lion patted Androcles with one of his good paws and licked him **affectionately**. Androcles stayed with the lion for several days to make sure that the paw was healing properly. Then the new friends said goodbye.

Androcles had only gone a mile or two before he was captured by Roman soldiers. The lion, slowed down by his sore paw, was also captured. Neither was aware that the other had been taken prisoner.

When Androcles was brought to town, his former master brought him to court. Androcles was **condemned** to die in the arena—to be thrown to the wild beasts.

The day came when Androcles, bound in chains, was led into the arena. The crowds in the stands cheered and cheered. Then, as Androcles watched helplessly, the emperor stood up and raised his hand. A hush fell over the crowd. The emperor dropped his hand, and a fierce lion that had not been fed for weeks was released into the arena. The lion charged at Androcles.

"My life is most certainly over now," Androcles said as he closed his eyes and waited for the lion to attack. Instead of attacking, the lion began to pat and lick Androcles. Slowly, Androcles opened his eyes. It was his friend from the forest.

"You showed me kindness when I was in trouble," the lion whispered to Androcles. "Now it's time for me to thank you and return the favor."

The people watched in silence. Never had they seen a wild beast befriend a human. "This man does not deserve to die," they cried. "Free him! Free him!"

The emperor agreed with the people. However, before he gave the command to set Androcles free, he asked that Androcles be brought to his royal chambers.

"You are to be free," the emperor told Androcles. "But before you go, tell me why the lion did not attack you."

Androcles joyfully explained what had happened in the forest and how he had helped the injured lion. Although the story was difficult to believe, the emperor had seen the lion's actions in the arena with his own eyes.

The emperor then issued a command that Androcles should be a free citizen of the land. He also declared that the lion was a gentle beast and should be returned to the forest to roam freely.

Using a story map   Turn to page 119 to complete the story map for "Androcles Meets the Lion." Look at the map to write a one-paragraph summary of the entire fable on the lines below.

_____

_____

_____

_____

_____

_____

_____

Check Your Understanding

Think about what you've read. Then answer these questions.

1. Why does the lion tell his family not to wander from the den?
    - Ⓐ He is afraid they will get lost.
    - Ⓑ He is worried that they will be caught in traps set by soldiers.
    - Ⓒ He does not want them to look for food on their own.
    - Ⓓ He thinks a storm is coming.

2. Which of these is a minor detail that does not belong in a summary of the fable?
    - Ⓐ A lion gets a splinter in his paw as he clears a path in the forest.
    - Ⓑ A slave named Androcles escapes his cruel master.
    - Ⓒ Androcles runs deep in the forest and then stops to rest.
    - Ⓓ Two hawks discuss Androcles as he sleeps.

3. In the fable, the fallen trees are compared to
    - Ⓐ slivers of wood.
    - Ⓑ matchsticks.
    - Ⓒ Roman soldiers.
    - Ⓓ twigs.

4. What happens just after the guards fall asleep?
    - Ⓐ Androcles escapes.
    - Ⓑ Androcles brings his master breakfast.
    - Ⓒ Androcles hides behind a mound of dead leaves.
    - Ⓓ Soldiers set traps in the forest.

5. Someone who is relieved probably feels
    - Ⓐ nervous.
    - Ⓑ weak.
    - Ⓒ unhappy.
    - Ⓓ relaxed.

6. In the fable, which clue word is a synonym for *camouflaged*?
    - Ⓐ mound
    - Ⓑ exhausted
    - Ⓒ hidden
    - Ⓓ certain

7. Why does the hawk say that the fate of Androcles is in his own hands?
    - Ⓐ Androcles has a secret.
    - Ⓑ Androcles is holding all his possessions in his hands.
    - Ⓒ Androcles has a sore hand.
    - Ⓓ Androcles controls his own future.

8. What causes the lion to moan and groan?
    - Ⓐ His paw is infected from the splinter.
    - Ⓑ He is sore from lifting trees.
    - Ⓒ He misses his family.
    - Ⓓ He is trying to scare Androcles.

9. From the details in the fable, you can figure out that Androcles is
    - Ⓐ a coward.
    - Ⓑ kind and helpful.
    - Ⓒ cruel and thoughtless.
    - Ⓓ very strong.

10. What does the word *affectionately* mean in the fable?
    - Ⓐ "in a painful way"
    - Ⓑ "like a hungry beast"
    - Ⓒ "in a frightening way"
    - Ⓓ "in a tender loving way"

11. Which of these is an important detail that belongs in a summary of the fable?

Ⓐ The lion waves goodbye to his family.

Ⓑ Androcles helps his master bathe and dress.

Ⓒ Androcles untangles himself from a leafy vine.

Ⓓ The lion asks Androcles to remove the thorn from his paw.

12. Which of these best tells the moral, or lesson, of the fable?

Ⓐ All creatures are thankful for kind treatment.

Ⓑ Think before you speak.

Ⓒ Don't trust anyone, including your closest friends.

Ⓓ Staying alive is more important than being free.

Extend Your Learning

- *Write a Fable*

  Write a new fable in which Androcles and the lion meet again. In a small group, brainstorm ideas for the lesson your fable will teach. Choose the idea that you like best and discuss the kinds of events that might help teach that lesson. Then write your fable. Keep in mind that a fable can be quite brief. You might want to reread the fable on page 116 as an example.

- *Continue the Story*

  Look back at the story on page 114. What do you think might happen after Tia cleans her room? Will she go to the space park to ride her autocycle? Whom might she meet there? What kind of adventures might she have? Use your imagination to answer these questions as you plan a story about Tia and her autocycle. You might want to use a story map to help develop setting, character, and plot details for your story. Use the story map to write your story and to create illustrations. Then share your story and illustrations with the class.

- *Retell a Fantasy*

  Complete a story map for a familiar fable, fairy tale, folktale, or other story you have read and enjoyed. Then design and create a book jacket for the story that will make others want to read the story. Use the details in your story map to write a summary of the story for the inside book jacket flaps. You may want to look at samples of book jackets for additional ideas.

Reading Selection One

Read the myth "The Story of Atalanta."

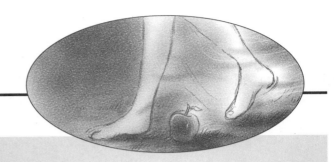

The Story of Atalanta

Zeus, the chief of the Greek gods, had a beautiful daughter named Atalanta. Atalanta was smart, brave, and strong. She was also a great hunter. Because of her beauty and skill, men were constantly proposing. Atalanta, however, was not interested in marriage. She just wanted to hunt, so she came up with a clever plan. She announced that she would marry the man who could beat her in a race. Atalanta ran like the wind. She knew no man could outrun her.

Scores of men signed up for the race. While they trained for the contest, a local young scribe named Hippomenes (hip-aw'-mun-eez) sat at his work desk, thinking about Atalanta. Hippomenes admired Atalanta's intelligence and strength of character. He believed that she would make an excellent wife. So he decided to enter the race. Hippomenes wasn't fast, but he was smart. Smiling to himself, he prepared for the race by slipping three objects into a small bag.

As the race began, Atalanta immediately pulled far ahead of the men. One by one, the tired men dropped out of the race. Eventually, only Hippomenes ran behind Atalanta. It was then that he put his plan into action. He reached into his bag and pulled out a shiny golden apple. Whistling sharply, he rolled the apple forward. At the sound of his whistle, Atalanta turned and saw the beautiful apple rolling toward her. She stopped and picked it up, astounded by its beauty. Immediately, Hippomenes sped past her.

Annoyed, Atalanta dropped the apple and ran easily by Hippomenes. After a few seconds, Hippomenes took a second golden apple from his bag and rolled it past Atalanta's feet. Again, she stopped to admire the beautiful treasure. Again, Hippomenes ran past her. Atalanta realized what Hippomenes was doing and she was pleased by his cleverness.

The finish line was in sight when Hippomenes rolled his third and final apple. When Atalanta saw the apple, she stopped, picked it up, and smiled. Then she stood and watched as Hippomenes crossed the finish line ahead of her. The next day, Atalanta and Hippomenes were married. Atalanta's plan had failed, but she was happy that Hippomenes's plan had worked.

Check Your Understanding

Think about what you've read. Then answer these questions.

1. In the myth, you can tell that the word *proposing* means
   A "annoying someone."
   B "asking to marry."
   C "entering a contest."
   D "hunting."

2. In the myth, Atalanta is compared to
   A a golden apple.
   B a hunter.
   C the wind.
   D the chief of the gods.

3. Which of these is not a detail used to describe Atalanta?
   A She was the daughter of Zeus.
   B She was a great hunter.
   C She was brave and strong.
   D She vowed never to marry.

4. How is Hippomenes different from other men who enter the race?
   A He trains harder and longer than anyone else does.
   B He uses his brain to form a clever plan.
   C He runs faster than anyone else does.
   D He wants to marry Atalanta.

5. Which of these events in the myth happens last?
   A Hippomenes whistles sharply.
   B Atalanta announces a race.
   C Hippomenes slips three objects into a small bag.
   D One by one, all the other men drop out of the race.

6. Why does Atalanta become annoyed during the race?
   A All the men except Hippomenes drop out of the race.
   B Hippomenes won't stop whistling.
   C Hippomenes speeds past her.
   D Hippomenes tries to trip her with apples.

7. From the information in the myth, you can draw the conclusion that
   A Hippomenes owns an apple orchard.
   B Atalanta is not as fast as she thinks she is.
   C Hippomenes is smarter than Atalanta.
   D Atalanta let Hippomenes win the race.

8. If Hippomenes plan had failed, he and Atalanta would have probably
   A never met.
   B not gotten married.
   C become good friends.
   D raced again.

9. The author wrote the myth mainly to
   A entertain readers with the story of Atalanta and Hippomenes.
   B explain why the ancient Greeks believed in gods and goddesses.
   C persuade readers to make a plan before entering a race.
   D describe an exciting race.

10. Which of these is an important detail that belongs in a summary of the myth?
   A Zeus was the chief of the Greek gods.
   B Atalanta said she would marry the man who beat her in a race.
   C Hippomenes sat at his work desk.
   D Hippomenes reached into his bag.

Read the article "All About Bears."

All About Bears

Many young children fall asleep with soft, cuddly teddy bears tucked under their arms. As a result, many people grow up thinking of bears as furry and playful. Teddy bears may be soft, cute, and sweet, but real bears are definitely not cuddly. They are dangerous wild animals.

Bear Facts

Bears are large mammals that can be found in Europe, Asia, North America, South America, and the Arctic. Except for the polar bears of the icy Arctic, bears usually live in forests.

Bears have large heads, short tails, and a shaggy fur coat. They have four short, strong legs with five-toed feet. Each toe has a long, sharp claw. Bears look clumsy when they lumber along, but they can run as fast as 25 miles an hour. They are also excellent swimmers, and most of them can climb trees.

Bears have powerful jaws with four sharp teeth for tearing food, and strong, flat molars for grinding food. Bears are omnivorous, which means that they eat anything. Most bears prefer meat, but they will also eat fruit, berries, and grass. And it's true, bears do love honey!

Bears prefer to live alone rather than in large groups. Many people think that bears hibernate, or sleep, the entire winter, but on nice days they come out of their dens to walk around. Bear cubs, which are born in the winter, stay with their mothers for one to two years. During this time, the mother bear protects the cubs from harm and teaches them how to survive in the wild on their own.

Kinds of Bears

The seven main types of bears are American black bears, brown bears, polar bears, Asiatic black bears, sloth bears, spectacled bears, and sun bears.

American black bears were once found throughout North America, but hunting and farming pushed them back into heavy forests. Black bears can stand as tall as 6 feet and can weigh over 300 pounds. Some black bears are actually brown and are called cinnamon bears. They can be born into a litter of black cubs.

Brown bears are found in Alaska, Europe, and Asia. The Alaskan brown bear, or kodiak bear, is the largest meat-eater on land! It can stand 10 feet tall and weigh 1,700 pounds! Grizzly bears are also brown bears. They can stand 9 feet tall and weigh 900 pounds. They once lived all over North America, but are now only found in some national parks in the western part of the United States.

Polar bears inhabit the Arctic. These giant bears can stand 11 feet tall and weigh more than 1,500 pounds. Their white fur provides camouflage on snowy, icy terrain. They also have fur on the soles of their feet, which helps keep them from slipping on icy surfaces.

Asiatic black bears live in Asia and have a white, crescent-shaped mark on their chests. Because of this marking, they are sometimes called moon bears.

Sloth bears are found in India and Sri Lanka. They move very slowly, so they are named after the slow-moving sloth.

Spectacled bears are the only bears found in South America. They live high in the Andes Mountains. They get their name from a ring of white fur around their eyes.

Sun bears are found in Asia. Only 80 pounds and 4 feet tall, sun bears are the smallest bears. They get their name from a yellowish patch of fur on their chests.

When a Bear is Not a Bear

Not all animals that are known as bears are bears. For example, koalas, pandas, and water bears are not true bears.

The Australian koalas are marsupials, a group of animals that includes kangaroos, wombats, and opossums.

The giant panda is a mammal that is found in China. At first, people referred to the panda as a bear. Then, for a while, scientists thought that pandas were members of the raccoon family. One type of panda, the red panda, is closely related to the raccoon. The more familiar black and white giant panda is more closely related to the bear. Today, most scientists consider the giant panda a bear, or a bear-like mammal.

The water bear isn't even a mammal! It is a microscopic animal that lives mainly in fresh and salt water and eats plants. Water bears are smaller than an eyelash! They have four short legs with claws on them and sharp, teeth-like structures on their mouths. It's not hard to figure out how they got their name.

Check Your Understanding

Think about what you've read. Then answer these questions.

11. Which of these statements is not an opinion?
    A Teddy bears may be soft, cute, and sweet.
    B Real bears are definitely not cuddly.
    C Bears are dangerous wild animals.
    D Bears are large mammals.

12. From the information in the article, you can draw the conclusion that
    A bears are afraid of heights.
    B bears are comfortable in water.
    C bears are very slow.
    D bears are found only in forests.

13. In the article, the best meaning of the word *omnivorous* is
    A "being very friendly."
    B "having sharp teeth."
    C "eating all kinds of food."
    D "having the ability to climb."

14. What can you predict might happen on a warm and sunny winter day?
    A A bear will wander out of its den.
    B A bear will go swimming.
    C Mother bears will leave their cubs.
    D A bear will hunt with a group of bears.

15. What is the main idea of the section "When a Bear is Not a Bear"?
    A Some animals that are called bears are not really bears.
    B Koalas and kangaroos are kinds of marsupials.
    C The giant panda is considered a bear-like animal.
    D Water bears are not bigger than an eyelash.

16. A cinnamon bear is a kind of
    A brown bear.
    B American black bear.
    C Asiatic black bear.
    D sloth bear.

17. Because they have fur on the soles of their feet, polar bears
    A never feel cold.
    B can run fast on ice.
    C are very slow.
    D are not likely to slip on ice.

18. How are Asiatic black bears and sun bears alike?
    A They both have a ring of white fur around their eyes.
    B They both weigh no more than 80 pounds.
    C They both have markings on their chests.
    D They both are found in South America.

19. Which of these details does not belong in a summary of the article?
    A Many young children fall asleep with teddy bears.
    B Bears are large mammals that can be found all over the world.
    C Bears are powerful animals that run as fast as 25 miles an hour.
    D There are seven main types of bears.

20. The author wrote the article mainly to
    A entertain readers with a story about a teddy bear.
    B convince readers to protect bears.
    C describe how mother bears teach their cubs to hunt.
    D explain facts about bears.